"Get ready for words to leap from the page into your life! *Father May I?* is a fantastic devotional journey of discovering more of God! I found myself laughing at parts and being stirred deeply just a paragraph later. This well-written book by Skye Wright is for you! It is a joy to read, full of treasures from the heart of a woman who is in passionate pursuit of God. Her journey will help you keep focused on what is most important in life. You will enjoy this book, so be sure to get an extra copy for a friend. They will thank you for it!"
    BRIAN SIMMONS
    Passion & Fire Ministries

"*Father May I?* is not only a refreshingly unique presentation of Skye Wright's journey into intimacy with God, it also beautifully and powerfully reinforces a much-needed truth regarding the role of the Father in meeting the needs and desires of His children. When I wrote the original article, 'Father May I?' published by The Elijah List, I had no idea that it would help inspire this beautiful book. Skye's story is very easy for Christians to identify with, and there's no doubt in my mind that anyone reading this book will be blessed and changed by it. So get ready to thoroughly enjoy this journey into the heart of the Father!"
    BEN R. PETERS
    Kingdom Sending Center, author

"Skye Wright's book, *Father May I?* is like a breath of fresh air. I want to call it 'simplistic beauty,' but I fear that the word 'simplistic' simplifies the impact it had on my heart. Skye takes complex truths along with real life stories and weaves them into a symphony that washes over the soul of the reader. I found myself captured and enraptured as she took profound Biblical teachings and made them tangible truths for everyone to be able to apply to their everyday lives. She truly turns the complex into the simple for each person who is privileged enough to read this book."

Kathi Pelton
Inscribe Ministries, author

"First off, I found my daughter's first book *Father May I?* a real knee-slapper! And secondly, delight-full; Skye's book and journey both. Watching you grow has filled me overflowing with delight. My Delight is In You."

Papa
Author of All

FATHER MAY I?

FATHER MAY I?

My 31-Day Journey of how You "Favour the Bold"
A simple book
Full of simple thoughts
From a girl
Discovering her Real Daddy

Skye Wright

Hillsboro, OR

Father May I?

Copyright ©2022 Skye Wright. All right reserved.
No part of this book may be reproduced or transmitted in any form or by any means, electronic or mechanical, without permission in writing from the publisher.

Follow Skye on her upward journey at https://upwards.ca

Published by Inscribe Press, Hillsboro, OR
Cover design by Pelton Media Group, Fredericksburg, VA
Cover concept by Skye Wright
Printed in the United States of America

ISBN 978-1-951611-33-0 (print)
     978-1-951611-34-7 (eBook)

Scripture quotations marked **NKJV** taken from the New King James Version®. Copyright © 1982 by Thomas Nelson. Used by permission. All rights reserved.
Quotations marked **NIV** are taken from the Holy Bible, New International Version®, NIV®. Copyright © 1973, 1978, 1984, 2011 by Biblica, Inc.™ Used by permission of Zondervan. All rights reserved worldwide. www.zondervan.comThe "NIV" and "New International Version" are trademarks registered in the United States Patent and Trademark Office by Biblica, Inc.™
Quotations marked **NLT** are taken from the Holy Bible, New Living Translation, copyright ©1996, 2004, 2015 by Tyndale House Foundation. Used by permission of Tyndale House Publishers, Carol Stream, Illinois 60188. All rights reserved.
Quotations marked **ESV** are from the ESV® Bible (The Holy Bible, English Standard Version®), Copyright © 2001 by Crossway, a publishing ministry of Good News Publishers. Used by permission. All rights reserved.
Quotations marked **NASB** taken from the (NASB®) New American Standard Bible®, Copyright © 1960, 1971, 1977, 1995, 2020 by The Lockman Foundation. Used by permission. All rights reserved. www.lockman.org
Quotations marked **TPT** are from The Passion Translation®. Copyright © 2017, 2018, 2020 by Passion & Fire Ministries, Inc. Used by permission. All rights reserved. ThePassionTranslation.com.

CONTENTS

FOREWORD	xi
PROLOGUE	1
DAY 1	5
DAY 2	11
DAY 3	15
DAY 4	21
DAY 5	25
DAY 6	33
DAY 7	37
DAY 8	41
DAY 9	49
DAY 10	51
DAY 11	55
DAY 12	59
DAY 13	63
DAY 14	69
DAY 15	71
DAY 16	75
DAY 17	77
DAY 18	83
DAY 19	89
DAY 20	95
DAY 21	101
DAY 22	107

DAY 23	115
DAY 24	117
DAY 25	119
DAY 26	125
DAY 27	129
DAY 28	135
DAY 29	139
DAY 31	153
EPILOGUE	171
PASSOVER 2021	180
ABOUT THE AUTHOR	189

DEDICATIONS

To Papa

"You are so much fun,
You are such a delight,
You are the Bright in my eyes
You are the Love of my life."
Discovering You has been My Great Joy

To Ernie,
To Terry,
And to all the fathers who left
And to all the fathers who stayed

"Great is Thy Faithfulness"

~ I honour you Fathers~

ACKNOWLEDGMENTS

First, I would like to acknowledge Ben R. Peters' prophetic word, "I Asked the Lord: Father, May I?" (https://elijahlist.com/words/display_word.html?ID=23542).

This as well as countless other words contributed to the conception and composing of this book. I think Katie Booth says it best in her book *The Invention of Miracles*: "At the time, the way that courts were considering invention was in flux, driven in part by the American image of an inventor as a lone discoverer, a cowboy, a hero. The inventor was always a single person with a dramatic breakthrough, whose credit was never shared. In truth invention was a long slog toward a quiet finish. Inventors built on the ideas of those who came before and built, too, on the ideas in the air, the whisperings of what other inventors were up to."[1]

We all know in part. But it was in the gathering of these parts that this book found its form, an even greater expression, a fuller sound.

And Brian Simmons, with his Papa Heart as well as Ted J. Hanson, a spiritual grandfather of sorts. You have shown me the Grace-Man and I can never go back.

A genuine thank you to Jeffrey Pelton, who likely unknowingly gave me one of my life's greatest compliments when he told me that I write like a song. Perhaps my dream to travel the world while leading worship looks more like the words in this book travelling the world through many different hearts. The sky's the limit!

And last but not least my husband.
You are God's Gift to me. The father who not only stays but who shows up, every single day, for all seven of our
One and Onlys.
"All Because Two People Fell in Love."

---

[1] Find our more at https://www.katiebooth.net/invention-of-miracles

FOREWORD

You haven't read a devotional like this before.

I am not generally given to hyperbole. In the business world, I endeavor to embody the aphorism "underpromise and overdeliver." It is always better to let your customer experience the joy of getting more than he or she bargained for. I follow that same philosophy in recommending movies, literature, sports teams, restaurants, paintings, cars, campgrounds…

You get the picture.

So, much as I might not wish to overhype this book by Skye Wright, I find it difficult to restrain my enthusiasm. I don't often read something that surprises me the way encountering *Father May I?* did. Daily devotional books aren't my regular reading fare, but I have read — or at least dipped into — a goodly number of them. And I tell you that the book you are holding, or looking at online, is a unique delight.

As a publisher, I receive a lot of submissions, and while I always appreciate people's desire to communicate the stories they have to tell, the truth is that "of making books there is no end…" (Ecclesiastes 12:12) so it is necessary to discriminate, which is a fancy way of saying "I have to be picky." This process isn't an art or a science; it is more like panning for gold. I sift through words to find stories that interest me, in a writing style that is clear and engaging and compelling.

In these days of social media, where people are convinced that every errant thought they have must be immediately conveyed and loudly expressed, we are inundated with a barrage of communication that is opaque, or amateurish, or ludicrous, or weird, or just plain boring. Unfortunately, it is easier than ever for that sort of writing to find its way into books. It can be difficult to discover an author who communicates with any sparkle or freshness or beauty.

Much of the time, to paraphrase Luci Shaw, one of my favorite poets: "Their words don't sing."

Skye Wright is an unknown writer — this is her first book — but if I have anything to say about it, she will not be unknown for long.

Her words sing.

When Skye first sent me her manuscript, with its funky styling and unusual fonts and partial sentences, I thought "Oh, here we go. I'll skim the first few pages and respond with a polite rejection letter."

I dutifully started reading. And I kept reading. And reading. And I laughed. And I was moved.

And I was delighted.

No — this may sound hokey — I was *enchanted*. My attention had been captured by what I immediately recognized as a fresh, quirky voice of a writer with fascinating things to say, and a fascinating way of saying them.

I wrote back to her: "I was caught quite pleasantly off-guard by your manuscript. It is different than the types of things I am generally interested in—but I believe you truly have a gift. You are a deep thinker; you have a firm grasp of your own 'voice'; you creatively weave your experiences into spiritual truth as little parables."

After reading through the book several times, I still feel the same way. I have been challenged and encouraged by Skye's insight and vulnerability and her innocent, seeking heart. I found myself viewing familiar truths through a fresh lens, a different viewpoint — as if I rotated a familiar photo ninety degrees and suddenly realized "Hey! This is more colorful when I look at it this way! And it's clearer, too."

That was my experience over and over.

Skye is convinced that God speaks all the time and he is continually offering parables and tokens of his love in all sorts of events — both large and small. Daily, she unearths treasures of the Father's heart for her and for those around her in the mundane day-to-day rhythms of life; although from Skye's perspective, there really aren't any "mundane" or "average" days. Each day, every moment, is an opportunity to glean more wisdom from her Father and receive greater understanding of his heart of love.

As you journey through these thirty-one days with her, you will be inspired to see *your* world with fresh eyes and delight in the riches God has hidden for *you* to discover — in his Word, in creation, in the events of your life, in his abiding, comforting presence revealed through little details everywhere you go.

Skye does not shy away from writing honestly about herself and her struggles and fears, as well as her triumphs and excitement and contentment. Through good times and bad, joys and sorrows, sickness and health, her love and commitment to her Lord and her family are evident and beautiful.

Through it all, she reveals the heart of a daughter who deeply loves her Father, and who is learning daily to trust ever more deeply in his faithfulness and goodness in her life. I know her prayer is that you, too, will be inspired to greater intimacy with our heavenly "Papa" to whom she has dedicated this love letter.

JEFFREY PELTON
Inscribe Press

A little background as we begin...

I have a print of a painting my mom bought for me just before this book came forth. It was given to me, completely unbeknownst by her, eighteen years to the day after I wrote the poem on the next page. This was not just any poem. It is the poem I wrote in Heather Clark's workshop at the Go School that she called on me to read out loud. The poem that was my heart in print at that time. The poem that launched the eighteen-year journey of my Discovering Father.

It is titleless, just as having no Father (I should say having no revelation of the Father) had left me nameless.

The print is of an eagle soaring through the snow, and it is titled ONWARDS. As she sat on her couch, having arrived home after purchasing the painting from the neighboring town where I was born and raised, she held it in her hands and asked the Lord what He was saying to me through this painting. And instantly, on the TV in the background, there came an advertisement for an animated feature about to be released called ONWARD. She knew it must be Holy Spirit. But it was when she heard the movie's "tag line" that she knew, without a doubt, it was Papa speaking to me:

"Whatever it takes I'm going to meet my Dad."

When I received the painting Holy Spirit told me to dig out that dusty journal and look up that poem. How marvelous to discover it was eighteen years previously — to the day. This marked my journey's end (or true beginning) and came directly on the heels of the encounter I had with Him when he called me away two weeks prior to a Valentine's retreat with Him. It was there I birthed faith. It was there my eyes were opened, my tongue unbound, and He appeared to me as He did to Abraham on Mount Moriah. In Genesis 22:9 (incidentally my room number was 229) it says, "they arrived on Mt Moriah." And vs 14 says, "So Abraham named that place Yahweh Appears. Even to this day it is said, 'On Yahweh's Mountain there is vision.'"

This book is my Eagle book. My Vision. My sight restored.

I remember the last day having breakfast and saying to Him, as I overlooked the beautiful valley and river, "I never did see an eagle the whole time I was here like I asked." And his gentle yet piercing response, "You are that eagle." When I saw Him I saw myself. Or at least began to.

All that to say that the eagle print gifted to me two weeks later is the picture that represents all the words in *Father May I?*

My ONWARDS journey ended and my UPWARDS one began.

    Is there a place for me
    Is there acceptance for my identity
Will you hold me if I push you away
    Do you know my deepest sin

    Is this my destiny
    Is my purpose here fulfilled
Will you love me if I fail
    Do you know my deepest pain

Will you withhold
The only thing I want
Will you deny me
The only thing I need

    When will I see My Father

02.26.02

(Disclaimer)

I believe God speaks through all of His creation. I most often hear Holy Spirit speak in nature and secular music and movies. When I quote someone, hearing God in them, it doesn't mean I share their spiritual or political views. When I quote a person, it is what I hear Holy Spirit saying that I am in agreement with. Enough said.

~Skye

~PROLOGUE~

04.30.20
For a few months now I have been hearing the word "ask" in the spirit.
And although I keep agreeing with what I am hearing I have not been practising it. This month of April it has become even louder.
Many prophetic voices posting Psalm 2:8.
And You bringing Jeremiah 33:3 to the forefront in my life this while.
Not to mention Matt. 7:7.
As I have kept putting off actually ASKING in this season I am beginning to see not only is it an issue for me, but it has been one for a long time. Trace back to needing to protect my Mom from the guilt and shame she carried at our poverty state I can see even as a young child I learned not to ask.
That coupled with the fact that due to growing up not knowing my bio. father, any no to a request was received only as further rejection.
It became much too great a risk and so I learned to not have needs.
Or that needs weren't ok.
Or that something wasn't ok with me for having needs.
It's all quite muddled but I do see I haven't been free, or rather safe enough to be a child. Confident in my Father's love, able to ask whatever my heart has so desired to ask.
Servants and slaves do not ask, or at least it is a rare occurrence. With sons and daughters asking is a right and quite an important one I am beginning to see which is likely why it was targeted by the enemy so young.
Now that I am being "reconnected" with my True Father.

Father May I?

(This, my 18 year journey. And this is the Hebrew month Iyar=connection.)

I am learning all I have access to. All that belongs to me.
So I thought for the month of May I would "practice" asking.
I may have had my asker returned to me but now I need to learn how to use it.
At the beginning of this month I was listening to a man connected to Bethel church in Redding, CA, a man named Dan McCollam.
He was speaking on wisdom and he answered something I have always wondered, esp. lately.
The question: WHY IS IT PROPHETIC PEOPLE ARE SO GOOD AT HEARING GOD FOR OTHERS BUT NOT FOR THEMSELVES?
And his answer: IT IS A LACK OF CRYING OUT.
It floored me. Simply floored me. I sat there stunned.
My first thought was it can't be; that's too easy! But then I looked back at my own life and could see the truth of that statement.
And I realized simple-yes, easy-no.
But all things get easier with practice.
Tongues. Driving a stick shift.
Leading worship in front of people. Times tables. Cooking.
Most things really do come easier with some repetition.
The more we do an action the less resistance we will encounter.
May has 31 days. So with this journal I will attempt to ask the Lord two things each day.
One question pertaining to more spiritual matters and one practical ask as in provision or physical healing.
I will document my journey and record my learnings and findings, my challenges and struggles, my victories and, of course, answers.
Some verses that speak of God being the One who ANSWERS...

> Matt 7:7 "Ask and it will be given to you." (NIV)
> John 16:24 "...ask and you will receive, so that your joy may be made full." (NASB)
> James 1:5 "If any of you lacks wisdom, let him ask God, who gives generously to all without reproach, and it will be given him.." (ESV)

Prologue

I Kings 3:5 "One night at Gibeon the LORD appeared to Solomon in a dream, and God said, "Ask, and I will give it to you!" (BSB)
Job 22:27 "You will pray to Him and He will hear you..." (NIV)
Jer. 29:12 "Then you will call on me...and I will listen to you." (NIV)
Psalm 91:15 "He shall call upon Me, and I will answer him." (NKJV)
Matt 7:11 "...how much more shall your Father who is in heaven give what is good to those who ask Him!" (NAS)
John 14:14 "If you ask Me anything in My name, I will do it." (NASB)
John 15:7 "If you abide in me...ask whatever you wish, and it will be done for you" (ESV)
Matt 21:22 "And all things you ask in prayer, believing, you will receive." (NASB)
I John 5:14 "This is the confidence we have in approaching God: that if we ask anything according to his will, he hears us." (NIV)
Romans 10:12 "...abounding in riches for all who call on Him." (NASB)
Eph. 3:20 "...beyond all that we ask for...."(NASB)
Psalm 2:8 "Ask of Me, and I will give You The nations for Your inheritance, And the ends of the earth for Your possession." (NKJV)

Even Esther and Salome had the king ask them what they wanted due to the pleasure they had found with the King.
Asking indicates an expectation of another's goodness towards us. When my child asks me to bring something back for them when I go on a trip, they are asking out of an expectation that I want to be generous to them.
When my child feels free to ask something of me it says I'm approachable. God is more than approachable.
We are instructed to boldly come without hesitation, never doubting God's good and generous nature, confident He is our loving Father who is so very pleased with us, His beloved kids.
So tomorrow it begins.

~May 1st~ * ~Day 1~ * ~2020~

Last night in bed I remembered, 'You have not because you ask not' so I looked it up. James 4:2 (TPT) says,

> "And all the time you don't obtain what you want because you won't ask God for it!"

And,

> "You do not have because you do not ask God." (NIV)

How many times I have been in a store and asked about a particular item not on the shelf and it's been in the back. I mean sometimes it isn't but often it is. I've learned to ask store clerks and shelf stockers, so surely I can ask My Good Father. I mean even Joshua asked for what would seem to be the absolute impossible and the Lord "heeded the voice of a man". Can you even imagine the sun standing still for a full day? How can that even be? And surely God could have won the battle so many other supernatural ways...angels...hail...disease...temporary blindness...but in this case he heeded a man.

What if Joshua hadn't asked?

Sometimes asking creates opportunity that a moment before wasn't even there. I know there have been times when my kids confidently ask me for something that wasn't even in my radar and it suddenly becomes a possibility because they asked.

And other times I am just waiting for them to ask for something so I can surprise them and delight them with my immediate YES or my precalculated genius idea or solution to the question or problem I could foresee coming.

So <u>how much more</u> does our Heavenly Father see what's coming and is all ready and positioned for our ask so He can yet again demonstrate and lavish His Goodness, His Extravagance, His Very

Father May I?

Best on us His Beloved Children, the Greatest Treasure of His Heart.
You would think that having a Father with unlimited resources and ability would make asking a non-issue.

> Matt 7:11 (KJV);
> "<u>How much more</u> shall your Father which is in Heaven give good things to them that ask him." (Underline mine.)

(Every time I see a 7:11 gas station or the clock says 7:11 or a purchase comes to $7.11 I am going to remind myself of this verse!)
I just love the words "how much more".
They are the language of the Kingdom.
I have been taking note lately of the Kingdom Language in Scripture.
Abundance. Beyond. Bountiful. Etc.
So to renew my mind, to subject my thoughts to God's "higher thoughts" I meditate on His Kingdom Language.
For His thoughts and ways are sovereign. They are above. When I come under them, when I bow the knee to His thoughts and ways, they can rule and reign in me.
They have supremacy.
So then I can see the issue here isn't my Father's thoughts or attitudes towards me that is causing this asking dilemma, therefore the issue must lie with me. The ball must be in my court so to speak.
This is the purpose of this 31-day practice which by the way I've already had an answer before I even officially began.
After James 4:2 came to me in bed I realized the 34+ hours of crazy high blood sugars my daughter with Type I Diabetes had been struggling with, I had taken on as my own problem to solve. This meant another sleepless night for us and blurry vision plus terrible moodiness for my 6-year-old.
And it hit me in bed as it was shaping up to be another long night (her kindergarten immunizations had thrown her body out of whack even more than usual) that I hadn't even once turned to Papa God, my own Father, and asked Him to intervene.
I had practiced Peace in His Presence, and Joy, and letting go which all had been effective in me navigating the current challenge

Day 1

in a good place and in a good way...but why had I not cried out for Him to help bring her numbers down?
It's almost like something in me learned a long time ago that I have to be strong (esp. for my mom who didn't have my bio. dad around) and believe it is up to me to face each struggle and challenge alone because it is for me to become more "Christ-like."
As I journal this I can see its absurdity and yet here I am.
What complex beings we are.
No wonder Scripture speaks of us becoming more and more child-like...meaning "like a child."
To leave the complex for the simple.
Simple trust. Care-free. Taken care of.
<u>Dependent</u>=keyword.
So I asked,
"Papa please lower Hope's blood sugars during the night" and by 5 a.m. she was single digits again and I actually got some much-needed sleep.
Thank you Papa. Thank you for hearing my request and answering it.
Which leads me to what Graham Cooke calls double-mindedness: I believe He can do it but will He do it for me?
There cannot be any doubt in His absolute Goodness towards us or else we aren't able to trust. So now we've come full circle.
You are fully trustworthy and yet I struggle to trust.
Lord let this month of "May I?" be the time you crumble every lie in me as the Person of Truth, every lie that prevents me from becoming child-like in my dependence on You and Your Goodness.
Free to ask whatever my heart desires.
Line my heart up with your heart, like Father like daughter, that I would be secure and bold in asking.
Thank you Jesus. Thank you HS.
I believe you are leading me in breakthrough.
So my 2 questions for Day 1:

(just start...harder than I thought...like staring at a blank canvas...)

Father May I?

> 1) Papa would you please REVEAL yourself to me, I want to ENCOUNTER You. We are in the Hebrew month of Iyar which corresponds with May and is when you REVEALED your Resurrected Self to your disciples as well as to the Israelites after Egypt as Jehovah Rapha.
> "I am the Lord who heals you." (Iyar is the acronym.)
> So I am asking for a fresh encounter with you that marks me during this month of May.
> Show up. Reveal Yourself to Me. Let me see My Father.

Which leads me to practical request #2...

> 2) Please heal Shelby's eye. It was injured and removed a couple of years ago. I ask you to cause it to grow back. (Shelby is my daughter's cat...the special cat that was born the day her older sister died.)
> Would you do a miracle with our cat?
> For my daughter's sake. For Shelby's sake. Because you can.
> Please fully restore Shelby's missing eye. I believe you are the God who creates something out of nothing.
> Perhaps this request fulfilled would ignite faith in the heart of this family to ask for and expect even greater things than a restored cat eye.
> In your name and expectant of your goodness I ask these things of you Papa-Amen.

*Just a quick note. As I was having that revelation last night coming into this 31 day challenge my husband was watching Star Trek Deep Space Nine and I happened to notice the episode title was "Favor the Bold"!
How fitting. Yes Papa! Make me BOLD. In other words instead of 'not having for not asking' let me discover your Favour in My Boldness!

later in the day

Just another two notes I wanted to document on my journey. Firstly Hope really didn't want to do school today (after such high numbers I don't blame her) and although I wanted her to do some,

Day 1

after a bit of pushing (which was then met with more resistance) I finally relented. She asked me repeatedly if she could please not do "school" so I asked if she'd rather paint to which she emphatically replied "Yes!"

I then realized 2 things:
1) It all happened because she was persistent in asking, and
2) painting was the better choice anyways.

After the fact I realized she was expressing a very real dilemma and it was within my power to help her find the "better" option. (Or in this case let her discover it herself.)

How much more is it within my Papa's power to intervene or provide "better" options that recharge me when I'm tired and just don't want to push through anymore. Although perseverance is something HS is always working in us, HS isn't a brutal taskmaster. How many opportunities for respite or refreshment have I passed by just because I assumed His answer or even what was best for me.

Def. food for thought.

And secondly I was all ready to head out and get groceries today (during Covid-19 quarantine) and my youngest son (14yrs) asked if he could come. Now I immediately said no as it didn't fit into my Covid-19 grocery plan but I felt a prompting to rethink my initial response because I thought 'my son just asked something of me'. The awareness of asking at work I suppose.

So I did rethink it and realized if he was willing to sit in the van while I bought food we could then swing by our fav. coffee shop that had conveniently just re-opened for take out orders and have a long overdue Mom/Son date.

And when I ran the idea past him he jumped at it.

Again I altered my plans due to a request from my child.

And the reason both requests touched me was because I could hear their heart in their requests and I was able to adjust to meet their heart need. One for relief and one for connection. Wow.

As we drove home from our happy time the story of the Prodigal Son came to mind; all the older brother had access to but because he never asked he never received.

Father May I?

He assumed the Father's intention was to work him and to withhold from him.
He assumed wrong.
Father forgive me where I have wrongly assumed your intentions, your very heart toward me.
Thank you that you are opening my eyes to see you as you truly are and for the freedom that is coming to me because of the Person of Truth in me.
I love you.
Amen.

~May 2nd~ ✶ ~Day 2~ ✶ ~2020~

Well just to comment on yesterday's entry before beginning today's, I've had what feels like 2 possible confirmations so far. One being that my phone notified me at 2:22 (Daniel 2:22) that Shawn Bolz (who usually represents Jesus in my dreams) had a short new clip released about a biker guy who had actually left the meeting and the word from the Lord for him was that, roughly paraphrased:

> 'This season God is going to give you a map over the calling you have, clear directions and instructions and you even came here to get those and you went home without them... it's because the Lord is going to visit you at home and speak to you about your future.
> I feel you're in a time between times, transitioning out of something and into a whole new place...a new place of authority.
> Be blessed in this transition to get the map from God in Jesus name.'

Now a few things leaped out at me:

> 1. I own and ride a motorcycle.
> 2. I have been asking God for clarity in my life
> 3. Maps are my thing...I have like 7 in my house...one is wall size
> 4. We are in between as we sold our 4-plex and don't know what is next but we know landlording is coming to an end

And most of all...

> 5. "God is going to visit you at home"!

I receive it.

Father May I?

This is what I asked yesterday Papa in this IYAR month of You Revealing Yourself.
"Show Yourself" Frozen II song just popped into my head.
Thank you Lord. Bless Shawn Bolz and team and I receive that word.
Confirmation #2 is Kathi Pelton's post yesterday.
The title: "May: A Month of ExtraOrdinary Grace and Help" with the Scripture Hebrews 4:16 following it:

> "Let us therefore come boldly to the throne of grace..."

Here are a couple excerpts that stood out:
> The Lord spoke to me that today begins a month of extravagant and extraordinary grace; GRACE UPON GRACE! He is inviting His people to come boldly to His throne of grace where you will receive mercy, grace and help for ALL that you need.
> In May we will see a great manifestation of the strength (power) of God being made perfect (manifest) in the midst of need (weakness). The power of God will rest upon you in ways that strengthen you, uphold you and help you.
> May you approach Him with bold confidence as we enter the month of May!

Makes me think of what I wrote yesterday, "Favor the Bold".
You are obviously speaking here.
So HS I ask you to empower me with BOLDNESS.
Boldness to approach you and boldness to make my requests known.
Makes me think of Esther approaching King Xerxes.
Now her courage is inspiring because she was dependent upon the king extending his scepter whereas you already have.
The veil is torn.
The way is made.
I can boldly approach at any time. Lord let that sink in.
Let me be child-like in my bold assurance that My Daddy is approachable.
How much more! Ha!
Wow as I finished that last sentence my Bible app just texted me today's verse which is, of course, so very fitting.

Ps. 46:1 (TPT)
God you're such a safe and powerful place to find refuge! You're a proven help in time of trouble-more than enough and always available whenever I need you.

More than enough. A Proven Help. Always Available.
More kingdom language to learn. To eat. To feast upon.
When I read that verse it really sounds like you are eagerly awaiting my request, my ask for help.
Thank you for this truth that My Father is Always Available.
For some reason that touches on something.
Perhaps my mom getting married just before I turned 6 and then having 3 more kids close together and her being kept quite busy in the natural has something to do with it.
She was such a good mom but of course I must have felt like I had lost the availability I once had with her.
So I guess this leads me to spiritual ask #1.

> 1) Today Papa will you please help my first response, when I find myself in a situation, be a bold request for help, confident you are ever available to help me.
> May I look to you first.
> Rid me of any and all lies that I have to figure it out on my own. The orphan mentality that says it's up to me.
> Break it off. Root it out. Bless me with this new default I ask in your wonderful name. Amen.

And now onto my more practical ask for today but first a note that I took a picture of Shelby up close yesterday to be sure to document her one eye.
Thought I should be ready.
There really must be a difference between the kid whose ask sounds more like a wish and the one whose ask is followed up by action such as a packed bag or a space prepared for a new item.
Ok well here it is:

> 2) Papa I ask you to cause all 12 sunflower seeds I planted yesterday to grow into healthy beautiful productive sunflowers in your Mighty Name I pray Amen!

Father May I?

Last Fall my sister gave me a prophetic word to plant 12 sunflowers come Spring.
Two months ago God reminded me of that word and revealed more of the spiritual meaning behind it...but I also felt compelled to take action in the natural as well.
A sort of confirmation of the spiritual. And I felt compelled to plant yesterday, May 1st, although it is likely 3 weeks too early.
We will see. I figure I can always replant.
I plant a garden every year but I've never done sunflowers before. I shall wait and see!

So to summarize Day 2:
You're my always available Father who is eager to help.
The scepter is already extended, the way made, and I am free to BOLDLY come to you "whenever I need you". Ps. 46.
Today I will meditate and chew on this truth.

~May 3rd~ ✱ ~Day 3~ ✱ ~2020~

Well...I had a dream about Shawn Bolz calling me up on my phone LIVE during a conference because I was on the DNA distant relative's sheet for two ladies he was prophesying over. He asked me if I knew them and I was like "No" and he said my name was on their list so he began to prophesy.
It was to the point. It was fast. And it was monumental.
It was like a clear map. Then done. But I can't remember it now.
Then afterward I saw him leaving the conference and asked him for a copy of the word. He said yes and asked for my # and put it in his cell. Over.
So funny how his biker prophecy came through at 2:22p.m.
I keep seeing 222 and 333 everywhere I go-for months now but esp. during Covid-19 and I know it's Daniel 2:22 and Jer. 33:3.
All about God revealing secrets.
The Hebrew month we've just entered-IYAR-the month of great revelations and understanding.
The month Jesus revealed Himself, His Resurrected Self.
The month of the Tribe of Issachar. Wow.
So before I get to my Day 3 "asks" some thoughts and confirmations since yesterday's entry...
I watched Brian Simmons LIVE study on Isaiah yesterday and Candice came on and was sharing her dreams hot off the press and what she's hearing God say for May and then they both prayed for and prophesied over those of us watching.
She said two things that stood out.
First was,
"This is a time of encounter with Him."
(Which brings me back to request Day 1!)
And she also said something like,

Father May I?

"As you press your heart into Him don't just ASK but be sure to listen!"
So Papa, let me take that to heart. Teach me to ask and listen both!
And then she finished with a Scripture and it felt so relevant to this 31-day journey.

> Isaiah 41:13 (NLT);
> "For I hold you by your right hand -I, the Lord your God. And I say to you, 'Don't be afraid. I am here to help you.'"

What a promise! I am here to HELP you! Makes asking so much easier!
So then this morning before picking up this journal I was checking Facebook and emails quickly while sipping green tea and waking up and my friend Beth had a post that caught my eye.

> 1 Kings 3:5 (NKJ);
> "God said ASK! What shall I give you...?"

Wow. Couldn't not include it here. I love how you speak HS - bringing pieces from all different places.
Like doing a puzzle by the cozy fireplace.
Or like going on a treasure hunt...on the lookout for the next clue. You are fun. The Kingdom really is Joy! Ha!
It's funny how just my 3rd day into this thing my mind is already starting to look for what could be my next request.
Not in a greedy way but in seeing opportunities and possibilities instead of seeing more proof or evidence of God not moving in power in situations and circumstances.
It almost seems like my inability to ask is rooted in the lie I have believed-that my Father can act but for me He won't. And the risk of asking is so great because a 'no' would equal rejection and so to protect my heart I don't ask.
But Lord you've been healing my heart so deep this past season. Eighteen years it took but now I see you.
I am beginning to finally know my real Dad.
I guess this is an area that needs dismantling and rebuilding.
So so thankful for what I heard Graham Cooke say yesterday during the 5th day of his quarantine course:

Day 3

"I will not leave you as orphans."
Those words of Jesus are to me, right now, like a healing balm as HS uproots lies and establishes Truth.
As I was just upstairs dealing with my daughter's low blood sugar all I could think about was how my Father WANTS to help me.
Like, I know this in my head, but it is going deep.
You are uprooting the orphan spirit in me, aren't you Papa?
Now I have come to the place of finally meeting you @ almost 38 years old after my lifelong search, my 18-year journey since my poem,
"When Will I See My Father".
Here we are. I have finally met you.
It took 18 years to make the 18 inch journey from my head to my heart but
    Here I Am.
      I see you.
        And now begins the delightful journey of getting to know you. And in turn getting to know me. The True Me.
And as I was meditating on how a Father loves to help FB notified me of a memory from 4 years ago.
It was a prophetic word I had posted by a Luc Niebergall talking about two rivers flowing from the throne. Rivers of fire.
One was "The Fire of Revival" and the other "The Refiner's Fire" and how Jesus said to him in this vision,
"You cannot have one without the other."
This part stands out loud and clear:
"The Refiner's fire comes upon the hearts of God's children to burn away the chaff of orphanship, therefore revealing refined sons and daughters."
So interesting. Also I just joined Keith Ferrante's free online challenge beginning the day after tomorrow called, "Unlocking an Abundant Mindset" and with it we all got a free PDF of his book. The entire thing is about breaking out of poverty thinking and coming into and living in ABUNDANCE.
Once again very timely as I journal this asking journey.
Everything always comes back to knowing the Father. Always.
The very purpose and mission of Jesus was to reveal the Father.

Father May I?

I love how James Jordan talks about how Jesus coming to the earth to die for our sins wasn't His reason for coming but how, in order to reconnect us back to our Father, He chose to die.
The cross is all about our reconnection with Papa.
What's really incredible is that as I write this I am reminded of Christine Vales's chalkboard teaching for this month of Iyar.
The Hebrew letter "vav" means nail or connecting pin and is equal to the number 6. Jesus spent 6 hours on the cross to reconnect us back to the Father. Incredible. Everything Father.
As all of this stirs within me I can't help but wonder at something.
Perhaps this 31-day journey is one of many "journeys" I will document.
And I hear the phrase "The FatherFULL Series" in my spirit which is interesting because I have grown up in (and a part of) The Fatherless Generation.
But something has changed.
I am now beginning to discover Col. 2:10-The Fullness of Christ in me blowing wide open the doors and completely opening up the way to my Father.
That I can discover and encounter MY FATHER and become FatherFULL.
No longer an orphan.
Wow. Ok. Long revelation rant! Now to my Day 3 asks!
Candice Simmons prophesied over me at the last TPT mentor's zoom meeting that I would be receiving cheques in the mail-meaning more than just physical cheques.

> 1&2) So Papa my spiritual and physical asks today are combined as I am asking you to reveal to me, at least in part, what "cheques" are coming to me (or have come) spiritually speaking-as well as: would you please have someone send me a physical cheque in the mail with my name on it specifically just as a confirmation of what you are doing in the supernatural?
>
> Please and thank you Papa!

What fun! You delight in responding to my requests.
Thank you - Thank you - Thank you.

Day 3

"Burn away any and all chaff of orphanship" in me once and for all Papa.
Once and for all.

~May 4th~ ✱ ~Day 4~ ✱ ~2020~

Elijah List today Lana Vawser posted Jer. 6:16 (NLT):

> "This is wht the LORD says: 'Stop at the crossroads and look around. <u>Ask</u> for the old, godly way, and walk in it.'" (Underline mine)

As I begin to ponder what my today's requests could be I find myself realizing I have had some things already that I haven't thanked Papa for.

For example, I thought of asking Papa for an encouraging prophetic word from someone this week as it doesn't happen very often...but then I remembered a man from the church I was a part of (until its doors recently closed) called me up about a month ago...Palm Sunday actually...and gave me a hugely encouraging word. So instead of asking for another one today I am thanking you HS- thank you Daddy- for that word.

I think I did thank you afterward but honestly I haven't thought about that word in weeks...and maybe I haven't just marvelled enough in what you've already said. Thank you so much.

You gave before I even asked. Wow. I am so blessed.

Don't let one word of that prophecy fall to the ground or through the cracks of my heart but with all of me I believe and receive the blessings and the promise you have given me in that word. Something good just around the corner.

Miracles. Healing for Hope.

Yes and Amen Papa! Yes and Amen!

The more time I spend journaling in this book the more obvious it is becoming that this whole 31 Days of Asking is in fact an answer to my prayer to be free of my Poverty Paradigm and Orphan Mentality. My "book of asks" in and of itself is an answer. Ha! Isn't that just like you Jehovah-Sneaky!

Father May I?

So today Jamie Rohrbaugh posted a radical prayer for writers; to release them.
She prophesied for the ready pens to write.
As I read and prayed her prayer I realized it is what my spirit has been crying out this season, esp. during Covid-19.
I am remembering a prophetic word spoken to me as a very young person...like 12 maybe...about a bursting forth of creativity that would shock everyone around me.
And I have been aware of this creative hovering presence just beneath the surface within me.
I believe it has always been deep inside-very very hidden-but now hovers just below the surface...like fish swimming in a lake just beneath the thawing thin ice...eager for its full melt and the fresh air it will give access to.
I have some ideas and maybe they're ridiculous or maybe they're greatly needed. Who am I to judge?
My 6-year old Hope and I spent yesterday's rainy Sunday afternoon painting on canvases.
I found so much delight in watching the dedication and resolve and sheer pleasure she had in creating and completing her picture. It is a large face with 6 butterflies overhead and she tells me with much pride that it is a painting of herself.
She is so proud and today Daddy is going to put it up in her room at her insistence.
At one point she happily said,

> "My painting is failing but it's not really a fail because I'm having so much fun. Right Mom?"

What freedom.
I've corked the creative process so many times because of the perfectionist tendencies that plague me. The lies that say if I can't be the best what's the point.
So I painted a purple sunset over the Isle of Skye and was so bummed at how miserable it seemed to turn out.
Nothing like my unrealistic expectations.
But I chose to rejoice in the process and esp. the quality time.
And whenever I began to feel like a failure I looked to my 6-year old daughter's example of Kingdom Childlikeness and I kept going.

Day 4

Well this morning I came downstairs and saw my painting on my way to my study and thought, surprisingly, how it actually isn't half bad.
And it made me smile thinking of our pleasant afternoon, so I grabbed it and brought it into my study; I too shall display it proudly.
And I have determined to allow it to bring me joy-imperfections and all.
Which leads me to my spiritual ask for today.
Last night I dreamed my eldest daughter went into labour and I was concerned because it was happening so fast and I didn't think she was yet fully dilated.
But since I had only ever birthed children of my own and not assisted others I wasn't sure what I was looking for...so I frantically began searching for help while she tried to wait.
Although that dream had another meaning for me, linked to my relationship with my daughter, as I am journaling about birthing creativity I am realizing it is relevant to today's 'ASK'.
Brian Simmons says most often when you dream of people they actually represent a part of you, so my ask for today is as follows:

1) I haven't "birthed" these things before (books, songs, paintings, etc.) so my prayer HS-the Ultimate Midwife, knowledgeable and skilled-is that you would help me birth this creativity hovering beneath the surface. Help me with the timing, knowing when to wait and when to push.

Please empower me from the birthing of a creative idea to its completion.

Thank you that the Creator of the Universe lives inside of me!

Let's do this together! Tandem! Amen.

~May 5th~ ✶ ~Day 5~ ✶ ~2020~
6:25 am

Well as I reread yesterday's juicy entry I am seeing I didn't get back to it and therefore no second request was asked. But I'm ok with that. Creativity fits both categories:)

Yesterday was Monday. I should have seen it coming as Mondays during Covid-19 with 4 school age children I am trying to feed, help school and just overall manage, ends up being a huge day.

All the work for the week gets posted and I get an overwhelming amount of emails I have to slog through and the kids always get a bit (or a lot) overwhelmed when they see the week's work all at once.

But before I launch into today, I do want to make note that I had a thought yesterday morning that I wanted one of my asks to be me hearing the Lord speak to me.

My ask was going to be about hearing.

As Papa has already pointed out LISTENING is a key part of this asking journey. And although I didn't officially write it down (as the day was so full from start to finish) I heard Papa speak to me so clearly.

I had a few hours of insane full-on 4 kids needing me constantly, I was multitasking to the nth degree (and I'm not a natural multitasker), and I was prepping food; all with Peace and Joy and lots of deep breaths.

My eyes were opened to see how this type of overwhelming scenario would usually take me out but instead I kept unloading the weight as quickly as it began to pile on.

Like a pot under pressure I kept looking to Jesus as my release valve because I knew none of it was worth fretting over.

And I was happy.

Father May I?

Happy my joy couldn't be stolen by the threat of unfinished schoolwork or the exposing of my incompetence as a Mother/Teacher. Nope. I didn't let it touch me.

    And then I heard,
        "I am so proud of you."

    And I was like,
        "What?!"

    and I heard it again, spoken with such love.
        "I am so proud of you."

And my heart was instantly warmed. And I realized He wasn't speaking about me getting it all done ('cuz we didn't) but about me letting it all go and choosing to rest in my identity in Him rather than in our progress.
Which, in turn, meant the atmosphere I was carrying kept defusing the potentially explosive situations I was facing.
So thank you Papa for speaking to me so clearly.
I love to hear your voice. I love to listen to what you are saying.
It's funny because a prophetic word came out right when I started this journal and it was about carefully guarding what you are hearing the Lord say in this hour and a warning that others would try to come alongside and say something contrary.
And for me, someone who looks for confirmations too often I'm sure, it felt relevant.
So I printed it out. By Russ Walden.
Well, then I was listening to a sermon a couple of days later and the preacher was all about how God isn't a genie you can just ask things of.
And immediately I felt like this journal was foolish and I was ashamed.
How shallow of me I thought. How unspiritual. How off track.
But then I remembered that word-the one that felt important enough for me to print (which I don't often do).
And I leaned into HS and I felt His reassurance to trust Papa and His process for me.
Although the message had a valid point it was not to be received as direction for me at this time. Why?

Day 5

Because God is teaching me to lean on and follow His voice.
My sheep know MY voice.
At some point I am going to have to start putting more stock into the fact that Papa speaks to me and I hear Him.
Printed word from Russ Walden:

> "The Father says today, this is promotion time for you. You are about to break the tape and win the trophy of a race well run.
>
> The heart of an eagle saint beats in your chest, and your time in the hen yard of religious poultry mongers is over! You have been one who has walked a long journey with Me, and I have seen that, says God, and I have seen your faithfulness when others have turned away. You are not a beginner in the knowledge of My kingdom. You have a hearing ear to receive My word and to apply it in faithfulness when you sense the winds of My Spirit blowing. This is a time for running the race that is before you on the backstretch of favor bestowed and strength outpoured by Me into your spiritual sinews. You will RUN the way of My commandments with fresh vigor and renewed endowment to be the champion that I have called you to be. As you run, there will be many on the right and on the left that will want to hand you something to drink of their thinking or give you advice on running the race-but the Father says, I am your refreshing. Do not allow others or their opinions about your choices to distract you from what I am purposing to do.
>
> There is a great tearing down taking place in your life so that I can do a great building up. I am doing a new thing, says the Father, so get ready. Put on your running shoes. Immerse yourself in my truth, and not the opinions of men for the opinions of men will not sustain you where I am taking you, says the Father. It is a serious time. It is a serious time, but also a time of blessing. Blessings you have waited on for a long time are on their way to you this day as you humble yourself and find a place of renewed cooperation with Me and My word in your life, says the Father!"

FATHER MAY I?

My Bible app just sent me this verse as I've been writing...

> Psalm 130:5 (TPT);
> "This is why I wait upon you,
> expecting your breakthrough,
> for your word brings me hope."

I love that.
I boldly come. I ask.
I wait upon you Lord.
Continually engaging in our relationship, worshiping, meditating, listening, knowing, believing, yes even expecting the BREAKTHROUGH that I know is coming.
I am to be in a posture of awaiting your response, knowing you hear my cry and love to come through for me!
This is WHY I wait-
Cuz I KNOW you'll come through;
What CONTENTEDNESS!
So ask today I want to hear you again.
Which leads me to today's requests:

> 1) Please speak a word or a phrase to my heart that brings me deeper into the reality of my identity in you.

And I do have a physical request.
It feels a bit strange, but it is in my heart to ask so I shall.
Favour the Bold.
My Gran had a plaque on her wall my growing up and when she died in my early teenage years it must have gone to one of her kids.
I haven't seen it since. But I remember it; there-on the wall.
My first 6 years of life I lived with her and my mom and my grandma- all four generations of women in 2 houses side by side.
Little did I know how significant the plaque was at the time.
An eagle. Isaiah 40:31. The prophetic call on my life.
The 18-year journey I have just completed of me discovering I am that eagle.
Well as I wrote down Psalm 130:5,

> "This is why I wait upon you..."

Day 5

I immediately thought of that plaque from over 30 years ago...I don't know where it went in the family and I can't even exactly remember what it looked like, but Daddy I ask you:

    2) If there is a way within your will to bring it back to me somehow, in some form, I would be very grateful.

Thank you that my earliest years were developed with that truth up on the wall of both my home and my heart.
You are so so good to me.

3:03 P.M.

Well I snuck in a walk alongside the river while out getting groceries.
Actually I told Papa we were going on a Father-Daughter date and that He was buying.
And then I giggled uncontrollably like a little girl...'cuz I remembered one of my kids doing that to me when they were younger. So proud, so sincere and so oblivious to the fact that I'd be the one footing the bill.
Haha!
So I got a Mocha Matcha with oat milk and honey (still missing coffee!!) which was surprisingly delish and drove down to the river walkway just to spend time walking together.
Not writing or reading or studying or watching speakers or reading prophetic words; JUST BEING TOGETHER.
I specifically asked Him to speak to me today (or rather that I would hear what He is already saying) so I felt drawn to spend time in our best connecting environment-nature!
Trees, water, Camas flowers in full bloom and all along the trail.
Loons, birdsong, sunshine, and a gentle May breeze. Glorious!
Me, Papa, matcha, and nature.
We just walked and talked but mostly walked, enjoying one another's company.
I caught a glimpse of my face in a vehicle window's reflection and saw a girl who was all smiles. Made me smile even more. Grinning like an idiot is the phrase that comes to mind but...it doesn't sound very Kingdom!

Father May I?

Anyways, all the while I was ordering my Mocha Matcha and was walking the walkway, I was intermittently humming a song that was going through my head on repeat. It was so subtle I would have missed it except there was a quiet and a stillness on our walk that allowed the space needed to hear the background noise and bring it to the forefront.

When I realized I was hearing a song I paid attention as I have learned when I hear a song in that way it is HS speaking to me. But I dismissed it at first notice because I had not liked the song when it came out in high school.

Back at the van, wrapping up our date, I heard it again even though I thought I had dismissed it so I looked up the lyrics and then I understood why I was hearing it.

First off: Papa has been calling me a "star" (like one that shines bright in the sky) for at least a year now...with countless confirmations.

Here are some of the lyrics[1]:

> ♪ Everything you are today is what you want to be
> So don't be someone else when you be the best so easily
> If you try and believe, my baby, you'll succeed
> And your eyes will make you see
>
> You're a superstar
> Reach for the sky
> And hold your head up high...
> You're a superstar ♪

I was quick to disregard what you were saying to me. Singing actually.

Help me to be more aware. Thank you for those beautiful words. The 1st line nails it.

I just want to be your pride and joy. And I am.
I just want to make you proud. And I do.
I can reach for the sky (limitless) and I can walk with my head held high (confidence).
Beautiful.

As I parked at the grocery store and headed toward the door I suddenly stopped realizing I had forgotten my grocery list.

---

[1] Released by Love Inc. (Songwriters: Sheppard, Degiorgio, Daymond)

Day 5

On that list is my meal plan for 3 days for 6 people and the needed ingredients. Without it I would be quite lost, overwhelmed once inside, and would quite likely forget a very main food item like eggs. I hate that.
And in that moment I thought of this journal.
How sometimes, in all the scatteredness of life, we need something itemized for us to give us clarity and focus.
It's important to know what you want.
I could just aimlessly roam the grocery store buying what looks good or stands out...but when it comes to preparing supper for 6 people I am going to need specific ingredients if I am to be successful.
Same with requests.
Being specific can be helpful and effective.
Like a kid's Christmas wish list or an insurance "proof of loss claim" where you list your losses. In both cases the Scripture 'You have not cuz you ask not' definitely applies! So yes. I think this is good.
And also how very key to have recorded your prayers as well as God's answers as a memorial of remembrance of the faithfulness of our Father!
How often does Scripture tell us to remember the goodness of God.

> Isaiah 46:9 (NLT);
> "Remember the things I have done in the past."

The Israelites used stones as a remembrance.

> Psalm 9:1 (ESV);
> " I will recount all of your wonderful deeds."

How many answered requests go unnoticed?
I don't want to miss one thing. Not one.

> And Psalm 77:11-12 (TPT);
> "Yet I could never FORGET all your miracles, my God, as I REMEMBER all your wonders of old.
> I PONDER all you've done, Lord, MUSING on all your miracles."
> (Capitals mine)

I remember so as not to forget.

~May 6th~ ✶ ~Day 6~ ✶ ~2020~
2:37 pm

Wow. Bit of a late start today.
Slept in and just overall tired this rainy Wednesday.
Just had a wonderful nap and now here I am.
As I sat down with my Peppermint Tulsi Tea and peanut butter energy balls (compliments of my daughter Roja), I checked FB quickly and saw a post, which is a repost from Dec. 2018, that popped out at me because of its description. It says,
"If you're struggling with a poverty spirit, this will help. One of my favorite prophetic words ever." and it is an article by Jamie Rohrbaugh.
I feel like rewriting the entire article but that would be very long so I will jot down that which stands out most.

"Prophetic Word: I Give You All Things To Enjoy"
   -"I WANT you to enjoy my blessings."
   -"It wasn't time for many things then but NOW IS THE TIME. So pray. Do the work in prayer that I need you to do to release Me to work and move in your life. Ask me for the rewards I seek to bring you."
   -"I am so willing, beloved."
   -"So pray specifically, but pray for the things to which you cannot attach words as well. Ask me specifically to do those things that you cannot imagine. Ask me even to put a gift tag on those gifts when I sent them to you, so that you will know which prayer each package came from."

> -"Petition Me to know Me and the depths of My love. My gifts are simply an expression of My love to you. They are not the only expression, but they are one expression."
> -"...generosity is who I AM. And my heart is to move on the earth AND IN YOUR LIFE with more generosity than you could ever imagine."

What an encouraging confirmation.
Esp. the words 'ASK ME specifically' like my yesterday post after the grocery store.
I love the line 'Ask me to put a gift tag on it...so you will know which prayer each gift came from.'
What an awesome prayer!
So Yes Papa!
I ask you:

> 1) Please 'Put A Tag' on each gift that connects to a specific request, that I know not only that it's an answer to prayer, but to which prayer! So great! (I guess there is my spiritual ask for today which is funny because sitting down to write I had no ideas for one! Haha!)

Well, this ask leads me to yesterday afternoon when I stole away in my study for an hour or two and upon entering immediately saw an envelope on my electric piano. My heart leapt like a little kid 'cuz who doesn't like to get mail?
I opened it to find a letter from my 6 year old that said, "I I I I heart heart heart heart U." Awww! And: "GIVE ME BACK MY ENVELOPE." Haha!!
My heart instantly melted. Flooded by the love of my daughter. She could have just said, "I love you", which she does, but I could sense her own delight in secretly delivering 'mail' to Mom, expressing her love in a new, fresh way.
The same message. A different expression.
It really rocked me. Still is rocking me. I have it up on my wall in my study. Except the envelope. She wants me to write her back. How could I not?!
I think my heart is raw and more sensitive going through this 31-day journal somehow. And more aware.

Day 6

I instantly felt I had somehow received an answer to my "cheques in the mail" prayer. I know it wasn't an actual cheque but it was mail addressed to me that found its way into my study and contained the highest possible currency known to a parent: the love of their child.
I feel HS did 'tag' this gift.
Jamie Rohrbaugh also mentioned in the same post that things may come different than what you expect. So amazing.
Help me not miss a single expression of your love in my life. I mean, not too likely, or I'd be too overwhelmed to function most all of the time as it would be so constant.
        A Continuous State of Overwhelming Bliss.
Jamie's article also got me thinking how gifts is one of the five love languages (Gary Chapman) and it is ranked one of my lowest. But is it?
Like, I sometimes wonder when we take those tests how accurate they are due to woundedness. Over this past season I've become aware that disappointments and hurts in the gifts department have caused me to repress that part of me. Hide it. Make it non-existent.
BECAUSE IF IT ISN'T A NEED I HAVE THEN I CAN'T GET HURT WHEN IT ISN'T MET.
Which goes back to not feeling like it is ok to have needs and wants.
So my physical ask for today:

    2) Would you restore to me the delight and expectation of receiving gifts?

And as I write this prayer I am reminded that it is Mother's Day this Sunday.
Gifts are not my hubby's thing so I've just let that part of me fade away, but I find myself with this strange urge to be blessed with a Mimosa in bed Mother's Day morning.
Where on earth is that coming from? I have no idea!
I've only ever had two Mimosas before but I suppose they represent a celebration of sorts.
So if I only wish it then it will only be wishful thinking but if I request it perhaps it will come to pass.

Father May I?

As much as I would love for the people I love to gift me with things I absolutely love, in reality, it's not going to happen too often. It has...on occasion. And I have loved those moments, those precious times I have been the recipient of a very thoughtfully surprising, delightful gift.

But sometimes it is just easier to know what someone wants. And it isn't selfish to say so. You have not 'cuz you ask not.

It's like when you're going through a hard time and people say the generic, "let me know if there is anything I can do to help" to like, ease their conscience from the fact that they aren't really helping.

I suppose those are the moments a powerful person would speak up and say,

> "Well actually gluten-free meals and some help with housework are the areas help would be most received right now. Thanks for asking."

Wow.

> A) If that was me saying it I'd be impressed with myself.

And,

> B) If that was someone I care about's response to my offer of help, I would be grateful to know what is actually helpful so I could act on it. If I could not cook gluten free or didn't have the time to clean, I could pay for another person's service.

I guess the point I am trying to make to myself is that not voicing our needs or wants clearly is really doing the people who care about us a huge disservice.

It is not needy to have needs. But let's steer clear of co-dependency here! Ha!

So I'm seeing today's second question really has 2 parts: Please restore to me the delight/expectation of receiving gifts, and I am going to put that into practice by asking my family for a Mimosa on Mother's Day with a simple breakfast in bed.

That would be splendid!

~May 7th~ ✱ ~Day 7~ ✱ ~2020~
6:17 am

As I am a week into this now, I'm beginning to find myself seeing another both/and truth in the Bible.
Like we aren't servants or paupers in the Kingdom so we shouldn't have to ask for everything. There is so much we have access to, as well as we are made to rule and have dominion, which I believe in part has to do with prophetic prayer declarations.
When I see one of my kids feeling insecure about who they are I speak confidence over them. I call their Spirit Man to rise up. I declare prophetic words and Scripture over them. I call things that are not as though they are. And I've been on this journey for years and still have so much to learn.
But in all of that there is also the reality that I am a little girl completely dependent upon her Father. And we can yell and declare all we want, (and to some effect I am sure), but if the child in me hasn't learned how to approach my eager, benevolent, and good Father I can't help but wonder if it's like putting the cart before the horse.
They say if you miss a stage of development in growing up you have to go back there at some point...
We are kings learning our authority and we are children learning our dependency. What a beautiful tension.
But I hear this whisper in my heart: "I am a child first. His child."
I ask today, Papa:

    1) That you would speak to me-Father to Daughter.

And oh boy, as I write this I am seeing a replay of the scene from an episode of a tv show I watched a few nights ago.

Father May I?

The grown daughter was leaving and her father takes her hand and looks her in the eyes and says, voice full of emotion,

> "You have made me whole."

And I am hearing you say it now.
Theologically I haven't a clue, but my heart has that familiar melting feeling that happens when you speak to me in that place.
I look at my own kids and feel the same way.
My heart of love is made complete by having children to love.
My children. They belong to me. They are of MY heart.
I will meditate upon your precious words to me, Papa.
Oh how your words to me are LIFE, sweeter than honey, better than wine.
I LOVE YOU PAPA.
I will come back later to write ask #2 for my heart needs time to ruminate a little.

3:50 p.m.

Well my sister sent me/us $50 for Mother's Day and our 17th Anniversary this Sunday (as it falls on the same day this year) just out of the blue. We don't do anniversary gifts in my family so I was very surprised when I saw the etransfer.
Can a surprise etransfer from my sister count as a cheque in the mail?
Absolutely. I'll take it!
I "see" the gift tag, Papa, and I'm so incredibly touched. Wowsers. How timely also because I had looked at a local menu last night offering Covid-19 take out for Mother's Day and I thought 'Oh wouldn't it be so nice if me and hubby could get some chicken curry on Sunday' but then I remembered our tight bank account and immediately dismissed the idea.

This was both an answer to my "cheque in the mail" ask as well as an answer to an unasked ask. A wishful thinking.
How good are you, that even in this asking journey you bless my "unasking." If that even makes sense.

Day 7

And to top it all off, my neighbour and I were talking on my after-lunch walk and he offered some of his lilacs to me for Sunday, as he knows they are our anniversary flower and how much I love them!
My heart felt so full as I walked away. Still does.
I set out yesterday to ask for a Mimosa in bed for Mother's Day and have so far received flowers and supper!
Being more aware of answered requests and the delight of gifts is helping me to SEE more of the GIFTS that you give me.
Like when you're pregnant and you start seeing a bunch of pregnant ladies or you buy a red car and then everyone is driving a red car.
My second ask today is:

> 2) That you would increase my AWARENESS and even prompt and inspire me to list them before I fall asleep every night.

I'm always telling people who think it's funny how I hear God talking through anything and everything that it's because I'm always listening.
Expecting Him to say something. Knowing He likely already is.
This is like that but in a different area.
My eyes, always looking for the many ways He declares His love for me day by day, moment by moment.
My dad posted Psalm 139 this morning and I read it then and it comes to mind again now.

> How precious Your Thoughts!
> ...How precious are Your Thoughts Oh God
> How great is the sum of them!
> Were I to count them they would outnumber the grains of sand!
> Every single moment you are thinking of me!
> You cherish me constantly in your every thought!
> (TLV and TPT vs 17 and 18)

Wow.

~May 8th~ * ~Day 8~ * ~2020~
6:56 am

What a beautiful day!
After a few rainy days it's finally blue skies and bright morning sunshine!
The birds singing so giddy and loud. They sing, content and cared for. Worms in the wet soft ground. Freshly made nests they've been working on for weeks. Free as a bird to be a bird, bringing joy to all with their birdsong.
As I am listening to one particular bird song I hear no worried tones, no anxious melody, no uncertain wavering tune.
My mind cannot help but go to Matt. 6:26 (NIV),

"Look at the birds of the air...".

The wonderful "worry not" chapter.
He must have had the intention before creating the world to use birds as His perfect visual and audio lesson for us in Matt. 6:26. Since creation, birds have been greeting the day with song, constantly as the world turns and morning moves across the globe. A never-ending chorus reminding His children at the break of day that as He takes care of the birds, He'll take care of you, freeing you up to sing your song.

    His mercies are new every morning
        So great is His faithfulness.
           (from Lam. 3:22-23)

I so needed the reassuring melody of His faithfulness this morning. Of His countless good thoughts toward me.
Last night was a bit of a rough one. We have our interrupted nights and then we have our rough ones. Tag-teaming nighttime care of our 6 year old with Type 1 Diabetes is big. On a good day.

Father May I?

Last night I became weary and woke up anxious and discouraged which I was able to detect by the words coming out of my mouth while discussing the night with hubby in bed early this morning.
Sickness and disease is such a heavy weight.
One we aren't built to carry. I know this.
Only one man's shoulders can take it.
Two FB posts this morning really spoke to me as I removed myself from my negative conversation and sought PEACE in His Presence. Oh, the glorious power of birdsong in the still of the morning.
One was my friend from Australia who posted John 14:14 (NKJV);

> "If you ASK anything in my name, I will do it."

Most every night when tucking my youngest daughter in I speak resurrection life over her cells, I declare she has the DNA of Christ, I cover her with the blood, I bless her body from the top of her head to the tip of her toes and back up again. Sometimes I pray a little in tongues, knowing HS knows exactly what prayer to pray.
I find it a challenge to live in the tension between believing for her miraculous healing and asking for the grace and wisdom to manage this condition well.
She is at one of the hardest ages to manage. Kindergarten/grade 1 growth and teen growth are apparently very challenging times, causing irregular blood sugars, not to mention her pancreas still spurts out insulin on occasion due to it only having been 1 ½ years. The cells that produce insulin have not been completely killed off yet as I understand it.
Anyways as I read the preliminary verses to John 14:14 (which I love-double # verse btw!) I see words like FAITH, BELIEVING, MIRACLES. Ask anything IN MY NAME.
Now I don't think that means just add in Jesus' name to every prayer-although I still do it...haha.
But a person's name represents their nature-who they are-right?
So asking and believing God for healing from the place of knowing He IS Healing.
IYAR- the Hebrew month we are in; also an acronym for the healing nature God revealed to the Israelites after leaving Egypt:

> "I am the Lord WHO heals you."

Day 8

Now up to this point my asks have been somewhat "safe".
About my own heart, my own stuff. Getting my feet wet so to speak.
If a cheque didn't come in the mail, not the end of the world. Right?
Safe prayers. Ha. Shouldn't that be an oxymoron?
But this one. This one is my child.
And as I'm trying to find the words to describe what it means that it is my child, I am aware that I am your child, and you know even more than I how your child is your heart.

10:37 a.m.
Me and my mocha matcha down at the river walkway.
The 2nd FB find this morning was Doug Addison.
He posted late yesterday with a big colourful background:

"PRAY FOR HEALING IN ALL AREAS."

I find it so interesting that I would stumble across that this morning out of all mornings.
FULL healing. ALL areas.
That sounds like Kingdom dialect to me. Full. All.
I don't ever want to settle.
Even the limitless meaning of my name 'Skye' is a constant reminder the ceilings have to come off!
Now. In this generation. No more delay.
I don't want to read another theology book on healing. Honestly I don't have the time to study and research all the previous healing ministries and movements nor do I have the desire.
I'm sure they are full of keys but Papa, I want to encounter you as Jehovah-Rapha in the month of IYAR. Their encounter with you as The Lord Who Heals must have been so very impacting for them to name an entire month after that encounter. That revelation.
I am reminded (thank you HS for your always timely and relevant promptings) of a time a few years back when my mom received a prophetic word by a prophet from Washington. And he was speaking to her about her children-all 4 of us grown-and he said to her:

Father May I?

"They call me Father."

And it was so impacting. For her and me both.
Her as a mother of 4 grown children and me as a mother of 3 grown and 3 growing children at the time.
I think as moms we so often mediate on our children's behalf that it can feel like God is our children's father thru us...almost like a grandparent or something. I don't know how to fully explain it but I remember the "aha" moment it brought.
So HS you are drawing this to the surface for a reason. Yes.
You are Hope's Father.
You are my Good Father and you are my children's Good Father.
And your desire for all of your children is full healing in all areas!
I believe it! John 10:10 ABUNDANCE!
2019 was my breaking year and at the end of it (1 year into Hope's diagnosis) I cried out that I couldn't carry it anymore.
It was the final straw and low blow, 5 ½ years after the death of our eldest daughter at 18.
I literally cracked open from the weight of it all.
And Papa, I remember when I cried out to you, finally, you asked me

"Why?"

and I was like

"Why what?"

And you asked me so gently,

"Why didn't you ask me to carry this right back at the beginning?"

And I was speechless.
I hadn't even realized I had never given it over to Him.
I took it on and like a trooper I pushed forward in faith, like a good strong christian should.
I went without a full night's sleep or even a half a night's sleep for a full year, my hair began to fall out, digestion issues flared up, and still I pressed onwards. I towed the line. I stayed the course.
I sometimes hate how much I relate to the older brother in the story of the prodigal son. Just saying.

Day 8

But then you revealed to me my vastly wrong assumption that it was my obligatory christian duty to just quietly carry whatever burdens come my way.
No wonder I broke.
What good parent would ever ask such a thing of their child. Seriously. Not one.
So in that moment of revelation brilliance I did what I should have done at the beginning: I asked you to take it. And you did.
Today I needed this reminder.

The JOY I have had these past 5 months of 2020 are unprecedented in my life amidst the interrupted nights and the sometimes challenging days.
A bit of a longer heavier entry today; hence the mocha matcha at my fav. journaling spot.
Day 8 of my 'Father May I?' journal journey. It's amazing how therapeutic this is.
I mean Lord, you know I'm an avid journaller, since I was 10!
Boxes of journals!
But a 31-day journey on a specific HS led topic is really quite adventurous and revealing and dare I say healing!
So in light of John 14:14, "Ask whatever you wish and it will be given" and Doug's new prophetic word, "Pray for full healing in all areas"; as well as the Scripture I have to insert here-the one that has been pursuing me relentlessly this month and this season: 3 John 2;

> "Beloved I wish above all things that you may prosper and be in health, even as your soul prospers."
> (KJV without the "th"s)

In light of these 3 rhema words I ask you today:

> 1) My Dearest Papa and most Precious Jesus for FULL healing in ALL areas for Hope and our entire family in the area of Diabetes. May her sweet 6-year-old body prosper and be in health as her soul prospers.

You are the God who brings the dead to life, so I speak "LIVE" to every place that has been attacked, beat down, despairing of life, unaware of your goodness, deceived by the enemy, destroyed

FATHER MAY I?

by sin, shrivelled up due to darkness, given up in hopelessness and defeat.
EVERY AND ALL PLACE(S) in Hope's BODY AND SOUL, IN OUR FAMILY'S BODY AND SOUL I declare "LIVE"!

> Ps. 118:17 (BSB);
> "I will not die, but <u>I WILL LIVE</u> and proclaim what the Lord has done." (Capitals and underlined mine)

He heals. You heal Papa. You are the Lord who heals me, who heals us.
Who heals Hope.
Psalm 103:2-4 (NKJV) says it best;

> "Bless the Lord, O my soul,
> And forget not all His benefits:
> Who forgives all your iniquities,
> Who heals all your diseases,
> Who redeems your life from destruction,
> Who crowns you with lovingkindness and tender mercies,
> Who satisfies your mouth with good things,
> So that your youth is renewed like the eagle's...."

ALL. ALL. ALL.

> This is the language of Heaven.
> Just her name alone. Hope.
> Our hope is in you and you alone.
> You are our HOPE.

Well, a cheque in the mail or complete healing from an incurable autoimmune disease ...which is harder for the Lord?
Creator of the Universe?
The one who knits bodies together in the womb.
I can feel the weighty hush in the van as I reread the declaration to live from the previous page.
Glory.
I am in awe of how you first revealed yourself to the Israelites as Jehovah-Rapha once they had escaped the bondage of Egypt.
I know we are in a Kairos time of the global church body crossing over. This recent Passover truly was significant.

Day 8

How important it must be for us to know you as Our Healer once we've left behind what once held us back.
(Or is knowing you as Healer how we let go of what once held us??)
My ask for healing today is both physical and spiritual but I will add to it this:

> 2) Please reveal yourself to me in a greater way, a greater measure, the areas you are already Jehovah-Rapha in our lives and the areas that you desire to be. As well as reveal any areas that have come into agreement with anything less than FULL healing in ALL areas.
> In your Mighty Name amen.

~May 9th~ ✷ ~Day 9~ ✷ ~2020~

Last night before bed Hope picked her Bible for story time. And she purposefully flipped to Joshua and the Battle of Jericho.
As I read it to her I knew it was HS speaking to me, continuing our conversation from earlier. About healing.
And although there was so much to it, the point I want to journal here is how they marched.
Day after day. With seemingly no results.
They didn't give up. They didn't give in.
To natural sight.
Like the line in the popular song "Waymaker":

♪ Even when I can't see that you're working
 You never stop working. ♪

So what a great visual for my prayer posture regarding Hope's healing.
Every wall will crumble and every knee bow and every tongue will confess.
Now we know in Jesus,
"It is Finished!"
So while I await His finished work to be made manifest in faith I keep marching.

Jericho was the <u>1st obstacle</u> the Israelites faced in entering the Promised Land right <u>after crossing the Jordan</u>; just like the bitter waters at the Wilderness of Shur was their <u>1st challenge after crossing the Red Sea</u>.
Both firsts correlate somehow, I feel, as I reread the story of Exodus 15:25 & 26 where God reveals Himself as "I am the LORD, your healer." (ESV)
This is the month IYAR.

Father May I?

The word Shur in Wilderness of Shur actually means to be up against a wall or hemmed in.
Definitely a connection to the other "wall" being Jericho.
I read online this morning a couple different Jewish Rabbis explaining how, although God heals all year long in the month of IYAR, He focuses on WHOLE HEALING. Really getting at the ROOT of our sickness or pain to bring complete healing.
Making bitter waters sweet.
My asks today are:

    1&2) For the bitters in my life, physically and spiritually speaking, to be made sweet.

Places I have forgotten.
Places I have ignored.
Hurts that have plagued me, words that have scarred me, seasons that have ravaged me.
I so believe we are in a season of restoration and new beginnings like never seen before.
I see 8's everywhere. 888. We are a family of 8 (correction, there are 8 members of this family still here on Earth). Like Noah's ark.
All the prophet's words of this time being like the days of Noah; our son is even named Noah. Another 2 names put together from 2 separate children make Rayne-Bo (Rainbow). We have a giant ark mural on our wall. There is no denying the significance "8" carries in our lives.
Open my eyes to see your restorative resurrection power at work in my life. Thank you in advance!
I am so excited for this season we are in.
What a GREAT time to be alive!

*Just an excerpt I found online to wrap up today's thoughts:
"Thus, the month of Iyyar epitomizes our journeys from darkness to light and our transitions from bitterness to sweetness. Another name for this month is Ziv (1 King 6:1), which means: 'brilliant light' or perhaps 'blossoming.'"[1]

---

[1]   I Am the LORD, Your Healer | Discover | First Fruits of Zion. www.ffoz.org.

~May 10th~ ✶ ~Day 10~ ✶ ~2020~
11:20am

17th Mother's Day, 17th wedding anniversary.
A mimosa and breakfast, dark chocolate and wildflowers in bed.
Only took 17 years. 17 is the number of victory in the Bible.
This is definitely a victory!
I instantly became a mother of 3 this day 17 years ago. When I said "I do" it was loaded. And at 20 years old. Wow.
A very well-deserved breakfast in bed!
I am so thankful I made my request for a mimosa known. It truly makes me feel special and festive. And interestingly enough, the joy it gave Hope and hubby (the other kids were sleeping obviously) to gift me with it made us all recipients.
When we won't receive we prevent another's blessing, for it really is more blessed to give than it is to receive...which if that were fully embraced in a culture there would have to be a whole lot of receiving going on.
Which reminds me of a quote out of my morning mimosa reading "The Abundant Life" by Keith Ferrante:

> "Giving and receiving are both critical to becoming a healthy resource person."

This morning sitting in my bed "receiving" my lovely gifts I experienced a bitter becoming sweet...
Raising 7 kids I wasn't able to have them climb into my bed with me at all young stages of development. Three were full-sized kids by the time we were married and our marital space was rare and highly protected.
(Esp. by my hubby.)

Father May I?

Couple that with moving into an open concept home just before giving birth to our 6th child, and our bedroom being a loft above the living room caused even less opportunity for in bed snuggles. Oh we snuggled tons on the couch and in their beds before bed and in forts and in tents and many other snuggle-available avenues. But my heart has had a hole from missing out on them crawling into our bed.

Well today, in lieu of Mother's Day and me actually staying in bed for once, as they woke one by one they made themselves toast and consecutively paraded upstairs to our loft and joined me in our bed and beside my bed on the chase...at one point the 2 teen boys had climbed into the empty jet tub (yes, a jet tub in our loft) and were both gaming on devices together.

That was quite the photo op!

But my heart swelled with JOY as I looked around my "room" and all 4 kids (the older 2 didn't make it home) and me and hubby squeezed into our "love nest" lounging, goofing, talking, squirming (6 yr old!), gaming (teenage boys), sharing dark chocolate together, just BEING.

And that place deep inside, that hidden bitter part, was revealed and healed all in a moment of time. Sweet as honey.

A Mother's Day I will forever cherish.

God you truly are good to your children. Thank you.

From this Mama heart to yours-Thank you.

And in this place I feel how dare I ask for more?

My cup runneth over.

But I will keep asking, I will keep receiving so I can keep running over-pouring out. For the sake of those around me.

When I am blessed my family is blessed!

So I ask for:

> 1&2) A confidence and boldness in mothering.
> With both physical and spiritual children.
> That I would confess and believe and live: "I am a good Mom."

My FB post today was an encouragement to moms to teach their children how to value themselves by demonstrating their own self-worth being put into practice.

Day 10

I want to OWN mothering my kids. Mistakes and all.
Take off all that pressure, the lies, that I have to do this perfectly.
What my kids need most is a mother who delights in being their mom.
I want to actually feel the shift in my home.
I'm a good Mom. I'm a great Mom. Ha!
Yes, the Mimosa was a GRAND idea!

    Confidence. Boldness. Courage. Fearless.

Like when my middle daughter said to my youngest daughter while playing bocce ball last night,
 "Can you please throw the ball like a normal person?!"
slightly exasperated with her 6-year-old sister's dramatic flair.
And my 6-year-old's response,
 "I'm not a normal person; I'm a FEARLESS person!"
I love that!
Fearless isn't normal. I want to be a fearless parent. Crazy confident.
Sure. Not in my own ability but in my position.
God has placed me here.
17 years in, it's time I own this!
AMEN! & AMEN!!
Now I'm off to enjoy another Mimosa cuz I can!

~May 11th~ ✶ ~Day 11~ ✶ ~2020~

I am in awe.
That Mother's Day was above and beyond what I asked for or imagined.
Not only was I blessed with my requested Mimosa and breakfast in bed but there was a vase of wildflowers, a dark chocolate bar, a lovely card, and the family all hanging out in my room which I already journaled.
Well after lunch my mom sent $30 to go toward our anniversary supper so between my sister and my mom that was $80, which not only covered the champagne for my Mimosa and chicken and lamb curry takeout, but there was also enough for a substantial tip which is always fun!
Blessed to be a blessing!
So that was more "Cheques in the mail".
Thank you Lord.
And then Roja and Boaz worked a couple of hours in the kitchen. Bo making the 4 kids supper as the takeout was adult only and Roja making dessert for me for a surprise. She made almond tart lemon curd! I was so surprised and overwhelmed by the thoughtfulness and hard work.
Mother's Day usually passes by with a card and maybe flowers or something lovely made at school...but this was full out.
Watching the family take such delight in blessing me...and it all began with me specifically asking for what I wanted.
What an eye-opener.
It is such a wonderful feeling to be celebrated. And so good as a mom to see my kids working together and excited about being a blessing.

Father May I?

Today I find myself faced with my next ask...as I step on the scale. Ha!

Two weeks ago I began a 7-week challenge where I asked my Mom and Dad and 2 sisters and brother if they would pledge $2 for every pound lost by my birthday-June 13th.

II called it the "13 lbs by the 13th Challenge".

They happily agreed. In fact this idea was part of what spurred the "Father May I?" challenge in the 1st place.

I am hoping to have enough money to get my hair done as well, as I needed some Covid motivation.

I felt funny asking and I kept putting it off, thinking it was a stupid idea.

But eventually I decided to take the plunge and ask...as my clothes were getting tighter by the day and I knew my hair would need some love after this quarantine.

Even though I knew that's what I wanted for my birthday-a fresh cut and colour-it was still hard to make my want known.

I decided to keep it light and fun and if they participated great and if they didn't have the funds, well, nothing lost. They could still cheer me on.

Well, here we are, day after Mother's Day, 2 weeks into the 7 weeks and although I lost 2 lbs the first week I somehow gained 3 lbs the second week! Oh boy! Thank you, takeout and tarts! And I'm sure the Mimosa and wine didn't help either.

So here I am 5 weeks left 'til my birthday and I have enough time still to make the challenge.

If I apply myself. If I can keep motivated, and if I can get a bit more active.

This is where my ask comes in:

> 1) Lord will you help me?
> Will you pour out your grace, that it would be easy and natural.
> Help keep my appetite in balance with my caloric needs. And I ask that this challenge would be both successful and fun!

By your grace I can be 13 lbs lighter by my birthday (and keep it off).

And on that note-

Day 11

2) I also ask you'd increase my hunger to read your Word and feast on you!

One of my favorite verses is Matt. 4:4 (NIV);

> "Jesus answered, 'It is written: 'Man shall not live on bread alone, but on every word that comes from the mouth of God.'"

Yes! I want to enjoy both. Natural and spiritual food!
Thank you Papa. Thank you for HS- Christ in me!
I rest in your finished work knowing I am already enough, already accepted, already loved just as I am.
Continue to teach me how to live out of health and wholeness!
In your Mighty Name - Amen!

~May 12th~ ✶ ~Day 12~ ✶ ~2020~
8:42 p.m.

Well I didn't get to journaling 'til now but my thoughts when I got up were about how it feels strange to ask for more...12 days in...like I'm selfish or greedy or needy even.
Then I felt like I heard,

> "If you feel like 12 days of asking is too much you really haven't got the point of this yet."

I went for a walk with my youngest sister, 1st time I've seen her in person in 2 months now due to Covid-19. She was talking about how she was out walking with an older and very wise woman from church yesterday and how she asked her about the story of Ananais and Sapphira as she was challenged by how they died. But what struck me was her courage in asking.
For all my life I have had a sense that questioning the Bible or God was doubt. Up until a few years ago I never questioned what I didn't understand in Scripture. I was thrilled to hear her experiencing more freedom in that area than I had at her age.
It got me thinking of children...how they ask so many questions trying to sort out and understand the world around them. And then you get a bit older and start to feel stupid when asking certain questions.
Like you should already know the answer.
It's almost like asking for anything means you are either dumb or needy.
I like this quote from Unlocking An Abundant Mindset,

> "The ability to ask others for help is actually a sign of health in your life...<u>People who see themselves as valuable speak up for what they need.</u>" (Underline mine)

Father May I?

I find having kids there are always so many needs...physical, emotional, and spiritual, and I can get quite overwhelmed at times in my limited capacity to meet all those needs.
I am often having to choose between needs: new clothes vs. sports, haircuts or vitamins, taking a much-needed hot bath or playing a family board game. I love my kids but often feel so limited.
Do I view you through the same lens Papa?
Am I looking from earth to heaven instead of from heaven to earth?
Look at this goldmine-Phil. 4:19;

> "And my God shall supply all your need according to His riches in glory by Christ Jesus." (NKJV)
> "And my God will meet all your needs according to the riches of his glory in Christ Jesus." (NIV)
> "I am convinced that my God will fully satisfy every need you have, FOR I HAVE SEEN the abundant riches of glory REVEALED TO ME through the Anointed One, Jesus Christ!" (TPT- capitals mine)

That doesn't sound like lack.
Funny, Shawn Bolz just posted on FB,

> "Sickness, financial failure, debt that will last generations and political toxic climates are not God's story for you. His story for you is John 10:10 life and life abundantly."

Life abundant sounds so EXPANSIVE, so generous.
Full of possibility.
Fear of lack results in hoarding and small mindedness.
Limited options.
I NEED **WHO YOU ARE** TO BE THE MOST DEFINING FORCE IN MY LIFE PAPA.
Thank you for this journey.
You are bringing me out into a wide and spacious place.
You know the way in this unfamiliar territory. I trust you.
I want to be so sure of your love for me.
Of how completely safe I am with you.
I want to just sink into the safety of your arms.

Day 12

To no longer clench my teeth. 37 is too young for these broken teeth.
The wrinkles, the broken teeth, the tired body that feels like 57... they indicate I've carried a weight too heavy for me for too long.
This past season has already been such a letting go...but I know you have more for me.
More peace. More joy. Heaven's language. More.
We've come so far- you and me.
So as my eyelids get heavy and this day comes to a close:

    1&2) I ask you for a dream.
    Speak to me as I sleep about how you care for me, how you take care of me, how you are more than enough and how I am absolutely safe with you.

Goodnight Papa.

~May 13th~ ✱ ~Day 13~ ✱ ~2020~
7:00 a.m.

As I was doing my morning quiet time I saw I received an email yesterday. It is Candice Simmons's word for the month of May. Interesting enough she writes Exodus 15:22 and about how she feels we have entered the wilderness of Shur regarding Coronavirus. She goes on to explain Shur means "a wall", "hemmed in", or "limited". She says,

> "We are in a place of restriction that's making it impossible to move forward without a miracle."

And then,

> "There is a realm of plenty just beyond our limitations. The end of your strength is the beginning of His."

This is just such a confirmation of Day 9's post.
Thank you Papa.
The walls are coming down.
Walls of limitation. Walls of sickness.
Ps. 103 (NKJV);

> "Bless the Lord, Oh my soul,
> And forget not ALL His benefits:
> Who forgives ALL your iniquities,
> Who heals ALL your diseases,
> Who redeems your life from destruction,
> Who crowns you with loving kindness and tender mercies,
> Who satisfies your mouth with good things,
> So that your youth is renewed like the eagles."
> (Capitals mine)

Father May I?

And I love The Passion Translation,

"You've healed me inside and out from EVERY disease."

This is Who You Are.
So I BLESS your name Yahweh.
You are So Good.
I don't remember having any particular dreams last night but if I do I will write them here.
Last night's entry is still rumbling in my heart...
There's the fact that I struggle to look to you to meet all of my needs and then there's also the fact that I feel the weight of having to be my children's provider-as if they were 2 separate issues.
But my children call you Father.
You are the Father of us all.
Who I trust with my kids truly speaks of who I can trust with my heart.
I no longer want the responsibilities of meeting all of my children's needs.
I am up against a wall. In my strength I am so very limited.
You knew this would be my Goliath, didn't you?
The wall of limitation upon entering My Promised Land and upon fleeing Egypt.
Upon both water crossings here is the wall.
DO I TRUST YOU TO SUPPLY ALL MY NEEDS AND MY FAMILY'S NEEDS?
ARE YOU ENOUGH?
YOU ARE ABLE BUT WILL YOU DO IT FOR ME?
The limitation of Double Mindedness.
As Graham Cooke said in his 5 day FB challenge at the beginning of May something along the lines of 'Double mindedness is believing God can do it but being unsure He will.'
ABLE AND WILLING.
That has always been my caveat.
I don't doubt your supremacy.
ISN'T IT ALWAYS HIS GOODNESS IN QUESTION?
O Lord, let that not be my story.
Let it be said of me that I broke through every limiting wall into

Day 13

the broad and spacious place of your ABUNDANT GOODNESS!
For my children and my children's children.
Yes, you knew this about me.
How aptly you named me Skye.
The Skye's the limit.
I have had prophetic words about how I am the only thing holding me back.
Renew my mind HS.
   I have the mind of Christ.
      With My God I can scale ANY wall!
         With My God the walls come CRASHING DOWN!
           With My God the bitter becomes SWEET because of HIS GOODNESS in my life.
Skye Wright, like the Wright Brothers, dreaming of the impossible:

~ FLIGHT. ~

I was made to Conquer,
    I was made for Adventure,
        I was made to FLY.

My spiritual ask today is:

   1) HS will you help me identify any limiting thoughts today that come up? And empower me to crumble them by Your Spirit.

And my physical ask is:

   2) That you would provide some new clothes for my Kids as they are all in need of a next size up wardrobe.

Thank you that you clothe the lilies of the field.
HOW MUCH MORE do you care about my children!

1:43 p.m.

Just got back from my walk and what a refreshing breeze, both in the natural and the spiritual.
I love the sound of your voice HS.
You clear the cobwebs.
You awaken my senses, making me more alive.

Father May I?

You cause me to breathe deep and open up.
A True Companion.
What a friend I've found.
As we walked and talked a couple of relevant things to this 31-day challenge came up so I'm gonna write them down while it's still fresh.
Thank God for screen time!
At the breakfast table this morning while eating yummy walnut apple cinnamon buckwheat porridge with homemade vanilla almond milk I heard the word EXPANSE and I immediately thought of the verse,

> "Of the increase of his government and peace there shall be no end." (Isaiah 9:7 NKJV).

To expand is really the opposite of to limit. To contain. To restrict.
Yes, limits restrict.
From Glory to Glory. From strength to strength.
Ever expanding. Ever increasing.
Now this is Kingdom language.
As we walked and I was delighting in hearing the word expand in a fresh new way I then heard the Scripture Gen 1:8 in the amplified version:

> "God called the expanse [of sky] heaven."

As well as Psalm 19:1 (NASB);

> "The heavens tell of the glory of God;
> And their expanse declares the work of His hands"

And as I write these I come across the verse God gave me when we moved here 13 years ago.
Isaiah 54:2 (Gods Word Translation).

> "Expand the space of your tent. Stretch out the curtains of your tent, and don't hold back. Lengthen your tent ropes, and drive in the tent pegs."

Again...my name...Skye...speaks to me of The Expanse of the Skye. I love that.
Also at lunch due to a slim grocery supply I decided to make curried lentil soup. Now my kids' palates have def. been "expanding"

Day 13

and changing over the years as I've grown in my health journey and esp. these past 9 months of being gluten and dairy free. They have come such a long way from what they ate as babes and toddlers but I was hesitant about lunch as I didn't hold back with the spices this time. It was truly a curried lentil dish. Not only did 5 out of the 6 people eat it but the pot was scraped clean and I was asked if there was anymore.
Now why did HS bring this to my attention on our walk?
The expand/expanse revelation-yes, very cool. Totally connected to my "limitless" prayer this morning but how is lentil curry relevant? Well I felt I was being drawn to the correlation between natural and spiritual.
Physically speaking lunch was a perfect example of how one can limit oneself.
First of all I didn't think they'd like it so I cut the recipe down by a third...turns out that limit was unnecessary- which originated really in my thoughts.
Second of all our diet has truly been ever expanding but esp. these past 8-9 years. By having an expectation my kids won't like something, esp. when they didn't the 1st couple of times I've made it, I am limiting THEM.
Their opportunities to grow and expand and get a broader range of nutrients and tastes.
HS was good to encourage me and remind me of how far I've come in this area. KD, tater tots and cereal were my specialties when I got married. Oh-and bagged salad and store bought poison oil, I mean dressing.
I mean if I look at what we eat now, and not just what we eat but the foods my kids cook and eat; it blows my mind.
But who's to say it has to stop here?
I often come up against a "wall" with our routine of meals only to find it causes me to push through and try some new recipes and flavours.
Some are a big hit and others take a while to develop a palate for. And obviously there's the occasional flop!
How cool to think there is always MORE.
More increase of His government.
More increase of His peace.

Father May I?

More foods to try, more places to go, new ideas and advancing technology.
I truly am my greatest limitation.

> "Change your thoughts, change your world"

is the wall decal by my front door.
And my own personal quote:

> "You have to think what you haven't thought
> To get where you haven't been
> You have to believe what you believed naught
> To see what you haven't seen."

It begins with dreaming it's even possible. IMAGINE.
The Wright Bro.'s had to first imagine flight before its innovation.

Oh, now I remember my dream last night, strange...
I dreamed Shelby's eye was beginning to "grow back" - I don't even know how that could be.
But now I've dreamed it.

~May 14th~ ✱ ~Day 14~ ✱ ~2020~
8:44 p.m.

I had a dream last night.
And it has been with me all day.
I have been putting off writing it down as I wanted to savour the sweetness of it, like a secret between lovers.
I dreamed I was standing in a room, speaking with a few people and a man walked up to our group and stood beside me. He was a head taller than everyone and his shoulders were twice as broad. And I immediately laid my head upon his chest. I couldn't not; it was like a magnetic force.
With no resistance on my part. I knew it was where I belonged.
With my head on his chest a feeling flooded my entire being. The feeling I've been looking for all my life. I was absolutely safe. I just wanted to stay there for always. There aren't words. It was more of an encounter than anything. And I have been relishing it all day.
If I could live from that place...
That is all for today.
I am still overcome.
This isn't just an ask; this is my deepest need.

    1&2) That I would live from the place of 'Absolutely Safe'.

So be it.

~May 15th~ ★ ~Day 15~ ★ ~2020~
6:48 a.m.

Day 15 wow! Almost exactly halfway. And HS just brought to my attention that this 31-Day "Father May I" journal challenge ends on Pentecost. May 31st.
That can't be coincidence.
This Passover, 2020, is so significant.
There is what you are doing world-wide in the body and then there is also what you are doing in my life.
The macro and the micro both.
And it's so key to be actively aware and participating in both.
Things feel intense. Like something's building...that feeling where the air starts to get heavy because a storm is brewing.
I planted seeds a while ago and I have been waiting for it to rain these past few days as the garden has gotten quite dry. The forecast called for rain the past couple of days but it hadn't yet happened.
The clouds were getting heavy.
The air thick.
I've even had a headache from the low-pressure system, but still have a dry garden. And by yesterday I was getting worried about my new little sprouts. They couldn't afford to wait much longer.
And then a strange thought came to me...just water them a little. Although I know it's rain they need as there must be something special in water that falls from the heavens that brings such life to the garden, to the growth. Everything brightens. Gets greener. Shoots up.
Ions or minerals or something.

Father May I?

But my thought was I'll water it so that it will rain.
Waiting and waiting is doing nothing.
But I remembered how numerous times-too many to count really-this has happened and as soon as I give in and turn the sprinkler on it rains and it used to annoy me.
But this time I did it intentionally. Why?
Well after I watered the garden gently I remembered my pastor, who is also my spiritual mother and sister both, saying to me once long ago that something has to be released down here before it is released above.
Like how water vapours go up from the earth to form the clouds that bring the rain.
And then I went for my walk, pondering this.
Could it be one of God's spiritual and physical laws?
That there must 1st be a pouring out from Earth before there is a pouring out from Heaven?
Wow. I instantly thought of the verse 2 Chron. 7:14 (NKJV):

> "If my people who are called by My name will humble themselves, and pray and seek My face, and turn from their wicked ways, then I will hear from heaven, and will forgive their sin and heal their land."

The water I poured out is what I had to give and I poured it out. I didn't withhold.
But instead I'm saying, Ok Lord, here's my little boy on the hillside lunch, here's my offering, here's my cry.
Whatever the "pouring", something is released up to Heaven that opens the floodgates, that releases the downpour, the multiplication.
Heaven's Response.
And as I walked it rained.
And by the time I got home it poured. And the garden and the earth got good and soaked!
Also on my walk my thoughts turned to the number 7 which is so very prevalent in this season. Both 7's and 8's are highlighted everywhere. As we walked the stories of 7x in the Bible began to pop into my head.
- Naaman dipped himself 7x in the water to be healed of leprosy.

Day 15

- Joshua and his men marched around Jericho 7 days and then 7 times.
- 7 times Elijah's servant checks the sky for clouds and saw one on the 7th time.
- 7 days of creation.

Here are a few more I am finding now...
- The ark rested in the 7th month.
- 7 years for Rachel, then 7 more.
- Hebrew servants released in the 7th year and rest for the land.

Leviticus and Numbers is full of 7's.
Obviously the 7 spirits of God, 7 lampstands, 7 churches, 7 colours in the rainbow, 7 musical notes, etc.
I could go on and on.
But the point HS was making with me was that the breakthrough, the completion, the miraculous happened on the 7th.

    7th day,

        7th dip,

            7th search,

                7th march,

                    7th month.

And HS spoke to me of rest. REST. 7 speaks of completion, perfection and REST.
That the breakthrough, the miracles, the healing, come when we finally enter REST.
LIKE MY HEAD ON HIS CHEST.
It is the alignment needed to receive.
All the way home on my walk I heard going through my spirit,

    "The Son of Man has no place to lay his head."

and a wise prophet from Bellingham spoke years ago of how that statement wasn't about Jesus being poor or homeless but about Him looking for a place to REST His Headship.
Just like after 7 days the dove was released from the ark and finally came to rest upon Jesus at His baptism, so is the 7-spirited God looking for a place to REST.
And when He can rest upon and in me and I upon and in Him; there is completion.

Father May I?

Perfection. Perfect alignment. Complete REST.
My 1st ask today is for REST both physically and spiritually.
Papa you know we haven't slept through the night in 17 months now.
The amount of stress it does to a body and brain is brutal.
We require rest. It is how you created us.
So I ask for:

> 1) Better sleep. For my husband and me. That we would both have our sleep restored to us along with more energy and clarity of thought.

Until Hope is healed cause her numbers to hold steady through the night I ask you. Please help us. We need you in this area, Papa.
We are trying and our efforts are failing most nights.
Come breakthrough for us in the area of physical rest. SLEEP.

> Ps. 4:8 (NIV);
> "In peace I will lie down and sleep, for you alone, Lord, make me dwell in safety."

And 2nd:

> 2) I pray any areas I need to lay down, let go and surrender control today, and in this season, show me.

Ps. 23:2,3 (ESV):
> "He makes me lie down in green pastures.
> He leads me beside still waters.
> He restores my soul."

I ask you—bring alignment.
That you, the head—Christ, would REST upon me.
That I would submit: come under your thoughts, your ways, your rule and reign.
That I would come into agreement with your Spirit in all things.
Today reveal where there needs to be adjustment and provide the grace to adjust and realign with you.
I ask in your All-Powerful and All-Mighty name Yeshua.
Amen.

~May 16th~ ✶ ~Day 16~ ✶ ~2020~
6:45 p.m.

Oh my. I just had a bit of a crazy wild thought.
What if everything I've asked for came true @ Pentecost?
How would knowing that change how I pray or how much I pray or what I ask for?
How would I pray if it were absolutely certain my expectations would be met exceedingly above and beyond?
Yes. I need this kind of faith Papa.
Or...if my prayers were answered as I prayed them...what's that verse...

> Matt. 6:7,8 (6,7,8-haha!) (NIV):
> "And when you pray, do not keep on babbling like pagans, for they think they will be heard because of their many words. Do not be like them, for your Father knows what you need before you ask him."

Wow. You already know.
Oh my.
What reassurance.
What Perfect Peace.
MY PAPA KNOWS MY NEED.
Today is about halfway...I'm going to take this day as a Selah...

~May 17th~ ✴ ~Day 17~ ✴ ~2020~
2:45 p.m.

It keeps coming back to walls.
The other day (May 15th) Russ Walden wrote:

> "You are a city on a hill, says God. You are the Zion of God whose walls the enemy cannot breach, or the thief cannot break through and steal. This is who you are in Me and who I AM in you. As I was with Moses, so I AM with you. As I was with Joshua, so I AM with you. The wilderness of confusion is not your dwelling place. You are moving this day into the land of Promise as I scatter the giants before you and bring down every wall of impediment that you might take the spoil and rejoice in the great testimony I have given you, even this day."

Walls that need to be up and walls that need to come down.
This whole Jericho/Shur thing has been about walls crumbling, overcoming obstacles, God doing miracles...but it's funny how much Scripture also speaks of rebuilding walls and how often these walls are named Salvation.
These walls must be very important.
I journaled about it May 15th in my other journal...thinking it was separate from this but after this morning I can see it is not.
Everything is always so inter-connected.
Our Earth's systems, our bodily systems, the state of our heart and our health...
Part of the healing that happens when the Lord reveals Himself as I Am the Lord Who Heals You (IYAR) is the rebuilding of the beneficial, even essential, walls.

Father May I?

I think of "leaky gut". Something I've been dealing with for many years.
A condition that is all about the walls of your gut not providing the much needed benefit and function required for health.
That is a wall I have been working on repairing for years. With some seasons having more progress than others.
So many conditions arise when that particular "wall" fails.
When our "walls called Salvation" are breached by the enemy...the result is suffering.
Something less than whole salvation. "Wholeness".
We become "compromised".
Well my sister came over for LIVE online church today and my kids have only seen her one other time during Covid so everyone was eager and lacking social skills and boundaries even more than usual.
It ended up being a very challenging visit with me walking my sister out to her car (at the end of the visit) so we could chat about how best to approach this dysfunction.
The more we talked the more I could see this truly is an age-old problem rooted in my upbringing.
Generationally speaking healthy personal boundaries are non-existent.
How can you teach something you've never been taught? So no shame.
But it's time.
For the sake of my children and my children's children and for my own quality of life.
Let's catch these foxes Papa!

> SoS 2:15 (TPT):
> "We will do it together"!

Really it is a root issue.
I feel we've come a long way in my identity in you, enough that hopefully addressing this weed doesn't threaten my roots.
For everything there is a season and truly you <u>are</u> restoring family.
I know it. I believe it. FAMILY IS EVERYTHING.
Restoration of hearts between fathers/mothers and sons/daughters.

Day 17

Now that I've come into a place of valuing ME how do I find the language needed to articulate my needs and expectations thus setting the appropriate boundary in my parenting, in my marriage and in all areas of my life?
I choose to not see this lack as failure on my part causing shame to thrive but to see it as divine opportunity-FOR SUCH A TIME AS THIS.
Your current struggle is your next miracle! Right? RIGHT?
With God on my side I can
   -scale any wall (overcome any obstacle)
    -nothing is impossible.
I will be called "Repairer of the Breach".

<u>Breach</u>= a gap in a wall, barrier or defense, esp. one made by an attacking army.

Makes me think of how many times the Bible talks about God being our shield.
- Gen. 15:1 "...I am a shield to you;" (NASB)
- Ps. 84:11 "For the Lord God is a sun and shield;" (NIV)
- Ps. 3:3 "But you, Lord, are a shield around me,"
- 2 Sam. 22:36 "You have given me the shield of your salvation," (ESV)
- Eph. 6:16 "...take up the shield of faith..." (NIV)
- Ps. 7:10 "God your wrap-around presence is my protection and my defense." (TPT)
- Ps. 119:114 "Your wrap-around presence becomes my shield..." (TPT)
- Ps. 62:2 "...his wrap-around presence always protects me."
- Ps. 5:12 "...you surround them with your favor as with a shield." (NIV)
- Ps. 125:2 "...so the Lord's wrap-around presence surrounds his people, protecting them now and forever." (TPT)
- Ps. 144:2 "He's my shelter of love and my fortress of faith, who wraps himself around me as a secure shield. I hide myself in this one who subdues enemies before me."

Wow.
There is so much about our shield being His WRAP-AROUND presence: SALVATION.

Father May I?

- Ps. 51:18 "Be the protecting wall around Jerusalem." (TPT)
- Isa. 26:1 "We have a strong city; God makes salvation its walls and ramparts" (NIV)

HS reveal to me your truth about how your SALVATION is the wall surrounding me, protecting me.
And reveal to me the "breaches" in this wall.
Places, areas where there are "holes" in the "wholeness" you've purchased for me.
Show me how to repair and rebuild these walls.
Relationally, with healthy Kingdom boundaries.
When my child speaks disrespectfully toward me and I have no response, when no boundary is enforced, it shows a gap in the wall.
A place where my worth, purchased and proven by your blood, is not valued by myself.
A weak point the enemy can use to invade and cause harm.
On both sides.
Walls are meant to keep out as well as to keep in.
Scripture speaks of the importance of boundary lines and the dangers in moving them, or in this case violating them.
And reveal to me your strategy for repair and restoration.
I ask for:

> 1&2) Revelation and transformation in this area of "walls": healthy relational boundaries. In my home. Starting now. I KNOW MY WORTH. Now help me walk it out I ask.

Thank you that you only ever reveal what you are ready to heal.
I declare I AM READY TO HEAL.
It is time for this breach to be fixed.
This wall to be repaired.
These relationships to be restored.
Let there be a marked difference even by the end of the week, in the way in which I handle myself and others when faced with disrespect and disobedience.
Help me say what I mean and mean what I say but not say it mean!

Day 17

6:10p.m.

On my walk I was praying about needing realignment and that led to me saying Ps. 51 and Neh. 8:10;

> Restore to me the JOY of your SALVATION.
>
> &
>
> The JOY of the Lord is my STRENGTH.

I was hearing don't limit God, you don't need respite, you just needed a walk in the rain with a bear sighting and to hear His voice.
I will write more on this tomorrow.

~May 18th~ * ~Day 18~ * ~2020~
10:07 a.m.

Yesterday late afternoon on my walk I was feeling a bit blah...my sister had just been over and it seemed to be one of those visits that brought out the worst in my family, socially speaking.
Having been 2 months in quarantine can't have helped!
I've been feeling it this week. Feels like the end of summer holidays.
Restless.
A lot of "together" time.
Must have been how Noah and his family felt after a while.
I was feeling a bit jealous of how my sister was able to call the ministry and tell them she desperately needed a break from the 2 boys she fosters and how they found her some respite so she could have a 36-hour break.
By the time I started out on my walk I had it fixed in my mind that respite was my only chance for a break and why doesn't the government help "diabetes families" who are burnt out and in huge need of a break.
Sounds a bit victimish, I know.
Well, by the time I got home I was in a completely different head space.
While I walked I experienced the perfect spring rain along with some intermittent sunshine.
It was so lovely.
The birds. The air. The wildflowers everywhere.
Then I stopped and watched a black bear across the river.
Just a little gift from Papa to me. He knows how I love wildlife.
And I realized I had been limiting God with how to refresh me.
I thought it had to look like "respite" but instead He had refreshment waiting for me in the form of a walk in the rain.

Father May I?

I could have missed it but thankfully I didn't.
Felt relevant to my whole "limits off" entry awhile back.
Then on my way home, feeling more peaceful, I was asking HS to help me come into alignment; get back on track-in all areas.
Diet, exercise, quiet time, school...everything feels "off", out of rhythm.
And after I prayed that out of my spirit came this Scripture out loud,

> Ps. 51:12 (NIV);
> "Restore to me the JOY of your salvation..."

and I was shocked.

> A) Why that verse? It hasn't been in my thoughts in ages.
> (Up until last night)

And

> B) It's about salvation.

This whole Walls of Salvation revelation yesterday.
His WRAP-AROUND presence-salvation-our shield.
Like a walled city, protecting us.
Keeping Righteousness, Peace, and Joy IN and the enemy OUT.
As I spoke out the verse I could see how it connected to the wall theme.
So I just walked with this verse on my tongue for a bit.
And then I said,

> "The joy of the Lord is my strength."

Yes.
When we are surrounded with His WRAP-AROUND salvation we have JOY.
His joy becomes our joy. His salvation is our salvation.
And we are strong when our walls are secure.
But when we are vulnerable and exposed, we are weak and joyless.
So then I go on FB this morning and my friend, Beth had posted this Scripture: Nehemiah 8:10 (NIV);

> "...for the joy of the Lord is your strength."

So so good!

Day 18

I also got an email link in the TPT emails I get called "Have You Had Your Miracle Today?" by Joan Hunter (May 11, 2020), and these verses stood out as I am on this asking journey with you HS...

- Ps. 31:19 "How abundant are the good things that you have stored up for those who fear you," (NIV)
- Ps. 67:7 "And the blessings keep coming! Then all the ends of the earth will give him the honor he deserves and be in awe of him!" (TPT)
- Deut. 28:2 "All these blessings will come on you and accompany you if you obey the Lord your God." (NIV)
- Luke 11:13 " If imperfect parents know how to lovingly take care of their children and give them what they need, how much more will the perfect heavenly Father give the Holy Spirit's fullness when his children ask him." (TPT)

An excerpt from Joan's article:

"When a parent gives their child a present, they hope that child will be appreciative and say, 'Thank you!' A grateful response will encourage another gift or surprise in the future. I believe the same thing applies to God. He gives and gives and gives to his children, but are his children grateful? Do they say, 'Thank You'?"

Then she says:

"Start a list today. Document every blessing or gift God has given you throughout your lifetime. Now, thank him for everything he has given you. Each of those blessings is a miracle!"

The thought I journaled yesterday during my "Selah" flows with this following excerpt from Julie A. Smith's word on Elijah List this morning:

"When you come out of this shut in, your Noah's Ark, what are your deepest longings and promises from God that you want to see fulfilled?"

Struggling a bit with motivation; day 4 of May long weekend...
I can see how key it is to ask, in faith, expecting Papa's response and action.

Father May I?

When I see my child doing what they can, unconcerned with possible future limitations and they come to a "wall", I will step in and work my parent magic wherever whenever possible.

When my daughter started swimming and wanted to go up a level and train more hours each week, she didn't have the resources to make it happen but she had the passion, the drive, to apply herself and the dedication to create the time in the week-even to the point of sacrificing youth group. And even though we didn't have all the funds I was able to work with the club and buy extra grocery coupons to go towards our fee.

I found a way because of her determination, her willingness to do everything she could.

How much more God.

When we show we really want something, like any good parent, He is eager to be the parent and do what good parents do.

Find a way.

But how many times is it we have an unmotivated child. One that looks ahead and sees obstacles so never begins. One that lives a life dictated by limits instead of one full of possibilities.

I want to expect Your Goodness at every turn.

I'm learning to ask.

I am becoming more aware.

But I can see my point of reference for provision is still "not being enough".

Or a fear of not enough.

Lack.

This is not who you are.

You are GOOD.

I know this in my heart more than I once did.

Now I need to know it more.

To the extent that I can be childlike in my abandon.

Unafraid and not worried.

Safe and a life without limits.

Is it obvious I'm feeling a bit off these past couple of days? End of period, looooong weekend, at home-still, losing (lost) motivation to "school", weight gained...blah.

I know, Papa, I could use some FUN.

Day 18

And I'll even try not to limit the form in which you can deliver the fun.
But please-you see me. You know it's been a long couple of months.
I ask for:

  1) FUN.

Would you infuse this moment in time with some great fun!
Surprise me!
Joy=Strength.
Fun is invigorating and refreshing.

5:10 p.m. after my walk
I'm not really even sure if my above 'fun request' is a spiritual ask or a physical ask but let's call it both,

  2) Double the fun!

Feeling still a bit off on my walk I began to list aloud the many gifts you've given me.
The many ways you've been faithful to take care of me. How can I not be grateful?!
Then I realized I need to go through the previous entries and list my asks.
Some of them may require my "preparing room".
Some may have been answered.
Some might require some partnering on my part.
I shall do that tomorrow morning!

~May 19th~ ✶ ~Day 19~ ✶ ~2020~
1:30 p.m.

Day 1
1) Fresh God encounter
2) Shelby's eye restored

Day 2
1) Look to You-first response
2) Cause all 12 sunflower plants to grow

Day 3
1 & 2) "Cheques" with my name on them

Day 4
1) Birth creativity
2) Thank you for previous word

Day 5
1) Speak a phrase/word into my heart-identity
2) Gran's plaque

Day 6
1) Put a tag on each gift
2) Restore the delight of receiving gifts

Day 7
1) Father-daughter talk
2) Increase awareness of gifts/blessings received

FATHER MAY I?

Day 8
1) Full healing in family in area of diabetes
2) Reveal areas you are/want to be Jehovah-Rapha

Day 9
1 & 2) Physical and spiritual bitters made sweet

Day 10
1) Confidence and boldness in parenting (both physical and spiritual children)

Day 11
1) Increase hunger for your word
2) 13 lbs by the 13th

Day 12
1&2) A dream

Day 13
1) Help me identify limiting thoughts
2) New clothes for my kids

Day 14
1&2) To live from the place of **ABSOLUTELY SAFE**

Day 15
1) Sleep/rest and steady #'s for Hope through the night
2) Reveal any areas I need to surrender in

Day 16 ~Selah~

Day 17
1&2) The healing of relational boundaries

Day 18
1&2) Fun! Double the fun!

Day 19 Today

Day 19

Wow. Honestly...I'm feeling pretty overwhelmed.
Papa I've called out to you very specifically these past 2 ½ weeks.
A lot of asks. Of a very wide variety.
From the healing of our cat's eye and daughter's diabetes to limits off and healthy relational boundaries to dreams and creativity birthed to cheques in the mail and clothing for my children not to mention an old Isaiah plaque from yesteryear and 13 pounds lost by June 13th.
Wow. It's actually quite the "eye-opener" (haha...that's funny, borderline cruel...) to see what requests have poured out of my heart during this challenge.
Really provides a glimpse into my heart doesn't it?
What's that verse...

> Matt. 6:19 (NIV);
> "For where your treasure is, there your heart will be also."

Where is my heart?
Am I drawing any closer to you along this 31-day journey?
Is this time well invested?
ULTIMATELY YOU'RE THE PRIZE PAPA.
TO BECOME LIKE YOU, JESUS, IS THE GOAL.
Like the question asked in one of the Kingdom Entrepreneur classes popping up on the internet during this quarantine:

> "If you could do anything in the world and money wasn't an issue what would it be?"

Mine is to lead prophetic worship
(where people encounter Papa's heart and are healed in worship)
all around the globe
(I want to see the world!).
Travel & Worship ~ Worship & travel ~ My 2 Greatest Passions.

So why is that the question that popped up right after I asked you where my heart was?
Are any of these requests making room in these two areas?
How much easier is it to ask you for clothing for my kids than for the deepest desires of my heart.
It's somehow safe to say I want more of you or take the limits off but the true desires of my heart?

Father May I?

That which I desire above all others but is seemingly so impossible and out of reach.

"<u>You are more than a restorer; You are the maker of dreams.</u>"
This is the prophetic word you spoke over my mom years ago.
I was at her side.
It was for our family.
It was for her.
It was for me.
It is for me now.
Why else would you bring that from the depths HS?
Clarity for VISION.
I see a home on our river property. A retreat? A home for healing?
How can this be when I'm such an introvert?
I catch glimpses.
But this is the year for 2020 vision.
To see and declare.
When the pieces begin to come together.
After all the years of preparation.
You have spoken this and I have believed you.
We have entered the 2 Sa. 30, Ziklag, "Recover All" ERA.
If now isn't the time to DREAM BIG then when is?
If now isn't when these longings start to be fulfilled, then what are we waiting for?
I turn 38 next month.
Last year, during my breaking year of 2019, I remember talking with my husband and we were discussing our need for vision and yet it just wasn't happening and he said something that I knew was you, HS.
He said,

> "You have to be able to dream before you can have vision".

And since then you've had me on a journey of discovering I am your dream come true.

GODs ORIGINAL DREAM

The Notebook (by Nicholas Sparks) quote you said to me on our Valentine's Day get away together-You and Me Papa-You said,

Day 19

"You are, and always have been, my dream."
And in the security of this place. Knowing I originated from the place of Your Desire...from this place I believe I can begin to dream.
What does it look like to dream with you Papa?
I don't want to live in the land of wishful thinking.
What asks are you waiting for me to ask that lead to my dreams being realized?
It's interesting. I have noticed in this last while Jer. 29:11 is EVERYWHERE.
More than usual.
With fresh HS highlighter ink all over it.
You don't just have dreams for me, you have PLANS for those dreams.
PLANS. GOOD PLANS.
HOPE is always about having a future, my sweet friend Marg always says. And it's true.
Abortion is rampant because there is no hope for the future.
Prov. 13:12 (NIV) says;

"...but a longing fulfilled is a tree of life."

And in TPT;

"But when at last YOUR DREAM COMES TRUE, life's sweetness will satisfy your soul."
(Emphasis mine)

I don't even know what my ask is.
Today's entry took an unexpected turn.
What must we do?

John 6:29 (NIV);
"...believe in the one he has sent."

Believe what you did on the cross was enough.
Believe you are good and have good plans for me.
Believe with God ALL THINGS ARE POSSIBLE.

We have a lot more hummingbirds this year and have spoken with many people who are saying the same thing.
Even my hubby, who isn't hearing God in everything all the time like

Father May I?

me, says God is speaking through this phenomenon and I agree.
The one thing I keep getting is that hummers are a symbol of God doing the impossible.
How they exist and maneuver and migrate; all of it-miracles.
One article I read calls them "God's Tiny Miracle".
This is the time.
To rise up in the earth.
Manifested-visible-sons and daughters of our Papa King.
Like Jesus. As Jesus. CHRIST IN ME the Hope of Glory.
I'm going for my walk now.
As we walk HS I ask you:

    1&2) To reveal to me one step I can take toward my dreams.
    Toward living fully as Your Dream Come True on the earth.

A shining star.
A city on a hill.
Your tiny miracle.

~May 20th~ ✲ ~Day 20~ ✲ 2020~
6:35 a.m.

I meant to journal right after my walk but then the whole supper bedtime routine happened.

As I walked your presence was so sweet and gentle. And you spoke to me of "INTENTIONAL DELIGHT".

I asked you what is the next step?

"What must I do?"

Your response:

> keep watching and marvelling at the little hummers,
> breathe deep the lilacs in full bloom,
> take joy in the different flowers all dressed in splendor.
> Be aware. Mindful. In the moment.
> Stay in awe.
> Be filled with wonder.
> Stay in the secret place.

COME UP HERE was what you spoke to me at the beginning of Covid-19.

And you brought me, through a dream, up a flight of silver and white stairs into your bedroom chamber with a window that overlooked the heart of the city. It was a place of much influence. It was the place of INTIMACY with you.

And I haven't cleaned or sorted my house like I could have in this time.

We haven't bitten into projects or busied ourselves in production. Like the line of that "Grease" song that I keep belting out loud at the strangest times (and now my 6-year-old does too!):

♪ You're the one that I want. Ooh ooh ooh. ♪

Father May I?

There has been a pressure in this time...
To perform.
    To prepare.
        To produce.
Launch online.
    Paint the house.
        School the kids.
Pray as a family.
    Discover a hidden talent.
        Rediscover yourself.
Heal your family.
    Create wealth.
        Get in shape.
Not that those are bad things.
Au contraire...when in the right timing they are life. Or the things of life.
Yet HS you seem to operate in "flow" and although there has been good things coming out of this quarantine it hasn't been because I've gotten busy.
Intimacy.
Surrender.
Remembering your faithfulness.
Counting the gifts.
And being thankful.
Choosing to stay in the place of encountering your goodness.
Believing I am who you say I am.
Believing you are who you say you are.
Meditating upon your words.
Holding close your promises to me.
Uncovering areas in my heart.
Rediscovering joy in your presence.
Singing new songs while we walk by the river.
Delighting in eagles and bears, hummers and wildflowers.
Walking together in the invigorating spring rain.
Looking for you, asking of you, leaning upon you.
This has been that season.

Day 20

You've drawn me into your presence.
The rest is up to you.

> Ps. 16:5 (TPT);
> "I leave my destiny and its timing in Your hands."

My Bible app just sent Rev. 3:20 to my phone as I was writing Ps. 16:5 out.
What's interesting about this is when He spoke to me so clear at the front end of Covid-19 that it was the season to 'Come Up Higher' (Rev.4:1) it was 3:20 that He highlighted.
I remember writing it in my journal and reading it over and over.

> You have been knocking
> and I have been opening
> and we have begun feasting together.

How beautiful Papa.
Is there anything else more important?
Part of me has felt the push to be "using this time wisely" by becoming a productive Kingdom Entrepreneur.
But this. Now. So precious.
Funny that reminds me of a dream I had last night. It was so bizarre.
I had this tiny baby. And she was so full of delight. And so was I. And our delight was in one another. It was such a force.
Powerful. I can still feel it.
It was so precious just being together; me delighting in her and her being full of delight.
Hmmmmm. So very interesting.
Every developmental stage is so necessary.
But this one.
Of being delighted in, fully taken care of and absolutely SAFE is foundational.
The core-the heart.
The heart is the Wellspring of Life.
Guard it above all else.

On my walk yesterday a bald eagle flew circles over me...following me as I walked home.

Father May I?

First he was low and with each round he climbed a bit higher until he was way up high, hardly visible anymore.
And it was like I was experiencing Isaiah 40:31 (TPT-capitals mine):

> "But those who wait for Yahweh's GRACE
>   will experience DIVINE strength.
>   They will rise up on soaring wings and fly like eagles,
>   run THEIR RACE without growing weary,
>   and walk THROUGH LIFE without giving up."

Experiencing waiting on you.
Coming up higher with each circle.
Perhaps my cry for that old plaque is actually prophetic of what you are doing in me right now, Papa.
Teaching me to wait on you during Covid.
Perhaps instead of needing the plaque I AM BECOMING WHAT WAS WRITTEN on the plaque.
Wow.
Which leads me to another interesting observation.
My prayer to lose weight...
I was sorting my journals a couple of weeks ago and putting the most current ones, 2016 and forward, in my study.
While flipping them open to see the date I opened to a dream I had back in 2016.
A very strange and short dream.

> I was visiting a church and the pastors were telling me all about how as a church they had all lost a bunch of weight together. Some church-wide weight loss program. And they were so excited.
> And then the pastor said something odd; he said;
>> "Yes, everyone has lost weight except the 37th person. For some reason they didn't, they were the only one."

What!
I would brush it off as a pizza dream, but I only write down dreams that feel significant. I realized I AM 37.
The **37th** person! Losing weight and staying healthy hasn't been an issue for me since having kids. I mean I go up and down a bit, but haven't gotten "stuck" at a weight.

Day 20

Until now.
I started gaining weight last fall. About the same time HS began speaking to me about Feasting. This is a season of feasting. I began to see licence plates everywhere I went with the words EAT and ATE.
So perhaps this is a feast season literally and spiritually. My natural world seems to always parallel my spiritual one-sometimes spookily so.
Maybe asking to lose weight wasn't the right question.
Maybe this has to do with rediscovering what a healthy appetite is. Maybe I need to gain back and then lose in the right places, in the right way. I was on a meat and veggie diet for quite some time and adding in some grains and more fruit has caused some of this added weight.
Maybe there is a redistribution happening.

    And a letting go of finding my identity in appearance.
    Another area I've had tight control over.

WHAT DOES REAL FREEDOM LOOK LIKE ANYWAY?
Wow. Ok, well, that was a lot of thought 1st thing with only 1 cup of green tea.
I think I'll go make myself a matcha, have some breakfast and chew on this emerging thought...that God's answers to my asks might be different than what I expected. Ha!
Definitely sounds like you Papa...

6:45p.m.

My ask for today:

    1&2) Would you remove that which hinders me from running my race. PHYSICALLY AND SPIRITUALLY.

Along my walk I kept thinking about bitter places-like Mara.
As hubby and I have had a rough two days it made me aware of bitter places in me. I don't have time tonight but tomorrow I want to add a word I read on FB before my walk on bitter roots...there seems to be a theme developing.
And my whole walk was me thinking about two of my life verses,

FATHER MAY I?

Phil. 3:13, FORGETTING WHAT LIES BEHIND and Hebrews 12:1 about REMOVE ALL THAT HINDERS.

That's my prayer Papa.
If this is the preparation season you say it is (which i believe you!) then ok.
Here I am.
As I weed my garden I am so aware of Your Presence-

~The Good and Faithful Gardener of My Heart.~

~May 21st~ ✱ ~Day 21~ ✱ ~2020~
6:55 a.m.

Oh my. I am in awe of you God.
How you direct and confirm.
How you speak to our hearts.
I was about to journal the amazing bitter roots post by Ted J. Hanson (an incredible prophet and apostle from Bellingham, WA, who faithfully sows into this region) as it so confirms what I've been getting about the Wilderness of Shur (wall) and bitter waters being made sweet.
But before I could even get back to his word I stumbled across Patricia King's post from 44 minutes ago and watched it and oh my.
It too is all about bitterness and preparing for Pentecost and at the end she speaks about Shur and Mara and how the Tree of Forgiveness CLEANSED THE BITTER WATERS.
How timely.
Yes, you have my attention HS.
She speaks of His sweet nature and how the spirit of Pentecost can't be poured out on bitter hearts and how key it is to position ourselves to be ready for Him.
Jesus you are cleansing the church. Getting her ready.
And then Patricia shares about Simon the sorcerer and how the witchcraft he operated in came from a bitter root.
Peter says to him Acts 8:21-23 (NIV);

> "You have no part or share in this ministry, because your heart is not right before God. Repent of this wickedness and pray to the Lord in the hope that he may forgive you for having such a thought in your heart. For I see that

Father May I?

you are <u>full of bitterness</u> and captive to sin." (Underline mine).

Wow. This is incredible. This is hindering me from running my race. P. King says bitterness and judgement opens the door to witchcraft, which can look like ungodly control, cursing, and manipulating, bringing hardship instead of blessing.

And how we need to put the cross in our heart that only sweet comes out of us.

This is why you revealed yourself first to the Israelites after Egypt as IYAR- I AM the Lord God Who Heals You.

You knew they couldn't enter the land with bitterness in their hearts.

Interesting how an issue came up with hubby these past 2 days which revealed a very sour, bitter place in my heart.

Some excerpts from Ted J. Hanson's post titled "Bitter Roots and Bitter Fruits":

> "Those bitter wounds have left us BOUND TO LIMITATIONS in becoming who God intends for us to be. If we are honest, many of our desires and many of the attributes in our lives have been shaped and bound by bitter experiences in our past or inheritances rooted in some bitter curse of despair. We must not be afraid of the bitter strongholds of our hearts and minds, BUT WE MUST FACE THEM and know that God's grace is sufficient to empower us to overcome in all things.
>
>> Joshua 10:7 So Joshua ascended from Gilgal, he and all the people of war with him, and all the mighty men of valor. 8 And the Lord said to Joshua, "Do not fear them, for I have delivered them into your hand; not a man of them shall stand before you."
>
> "When Joshua pursued his enemy, the Lord fought with him in a supernatural way. When we stand to overcome the things of bitterness that resist us from being who we are meant to be in Christ, WE CAN EXPECT THAT GOD WILL FIGHT WITH US IN A SUPERNATURAL WAY. This is the testimony of grace!"

Day 21

And then at the bottom of his blog he ends with this:

> "In the battle, Joshua put these kings in a cave and when thebattle was complete, he called the next generation to put their feet on the necks of these kings. GOD WANTS TO EMPOWER AN EMERGING GENERATION TO STAND IN THE VICTORY OVER THE BITTER ROOTS OF THE PAST. This is essential to becoming the body of Christ that stands to bring life to the world."
> (Emphasis mine)

Interesting about Joshua 10:11 (NIV);

> "As they fled ...the Lord hurled large hailstones down on them, and more of them died from the hail than were killed by the swords of the Israelites."

I have noticed we have had more hail than usual this past month... and large! And according to Dr. Brian Simmons hail is a symbol of God judging a stronghold of lies (Isaiah 28:17).
And then in my email this morning from TPT:

> (Excerpts from "I Hear His Whisper...My love restores you.")

> "I will restore you. Never limit Me. I will restore your family and those you love. All will know that I am the One who gives back to you what has been lost. Don't doubt My grace that is enough for you and for your family.

> "I will restore your mind and your heart as you come before Me. Crooked things will be made straight within you, healing your spirit, and soothing your soul.

> "I will restore your dreams. I will fulfill those desires within you and bring them to completion."

And the verse posted in my email to go with that is none other than

> Ps. 51:12 (TPT):
> "Let my passion for life be restored, tasting joy in every breakthrough you bring to me."

Restore unto me the JOY of Your Salvation.

Father May I?

Yes.
I see the connection.
Bitterness prevents JOY.
Salvation = healing.
The tree cast into the bitter waters of Mara making it sweet.
The JOY of our Wall of Salvation; your forgiveness that protects us and our forgiveness that protects us.
Keeping JOY in and bitterness out.
There are bitter roots in my heart aren't there, Papa?
Preventing me from running UNHINDERED.
Cracks in the walls stealing my JOY.
I cannot help but think of my sister who, in her younger years had so much bitterness in her heart toward our brother. And how she completely transformed after she encountered you, Papa, at a youth conference. As she released all the bitter tears you came in your sweetness and healed her heart as she forgave. And they became the best of friends and are super close still.
It was a once-and-for-all moment.
An encounter where the tree met the bitter water.
Like how King Hezekiah, in Isaiah chapter 38, wept bitter tears but was then healed.

My spiritual ask:
1) Would you help me posture myself, as we approach Pentecost, to receive healing from any and all bitter places in my heart?

I keep seeing 2 pictures.
One is a scene from a tv show a couple of weeks ago where the main character gets bitten by a snake and his entire leg gets infected and it begins to spread to his entire body to the point of needing amputation or he will die.
And the 2nd is the Israelites in the wilderness being bitten by snakes and having to "look up" to the bronze snake on the cross.
Both pictures reveal the poison of a snake bite entering the body and spreading throughout the body resulting in death.
Because the poison doesn't stay localized.

Day 21

I think Hebrews says that a bitter root defiles many.
Well, that could be taken to mean many parts of the body.
It spreads. Such is the nature of bitterness.
In the tv episode it required an antibiotic injection directly into the wound to save the man's leg.
For the Israelites it took lifting their eyes to the prophetic "cross".
And for Mara's bitter waters it took a tree.
In the case of bitter's poison an antidote is required.
A counter measure.
It doesn't just heal with time.
The poison must be purged. Eradicated. Removed.

My 2nd ask is:

   2) Physically speaking, please bring someone into my path I can bless. Whisper to me so I know who you are highlighting. Help me to move in the opposite spirit even in the natural Papa.

Because a bitter heart can't be a generous giver.
And you've been so very generous to me.
Thank you for your sweetness Jesus.
MAY IT PERMEATE EVERY PART OF ME.
      From my head to my toes.
      From my heart to my body.
      Everything made sweet by you.
          Amen.

~May 22nd~ * ~Day 22~ * ~2020~

Just an interesting note to add to yesterday's theme of bitterness and healing.
I have been aware of my 38th birthday coming up next month.
Numbers are such a significant part of my hearing from God.
There is always a chapter in the Bible that corresponds with how old I am turning and it applies for the whole year.
Now it's often a psalm but not always.
This year it has been Psalm 37.
A few excerpts from the Passion Translation that have really spoken to my heart all year:

> V3 "Fix your heart on the promises of God and you will be secure, feasting on his faithfulness."
>
> V4 "Make God the utmost delight and pleasure of your life and he will provide for you what you desire the most."
>
> V9 "Those who trust in the Lord will live safe and sound with blessings overflowing."
>
> V17 "For the Lord takes care of all his forgiven ones."
>
> V19 "Even in a time of disaster he will watch over them and they will always have more than enough no matter what happens."
>
> V25,26 "Not once have I found a lover of God forsaken by him, nor have any of their children gone hungry. Instead, I've found the godly ones to be the generous ones who give freely to others. Their children are blessed and become a blessing."
>
> V28 "They will be kept forever in his faithful care."

Father May I?

> V37 (37:37) "The godly ones will have a peaceful, prosperous future with a happy ending."
>
> V40 "Because of their faith in him, their daily portion will be a Father's help and deliverance from evil."

Wow. Just rereading it now, in light of this journal, I am in awe of how much this psalm has to do with all I've been writing.
Safe and sound.
Blessings overflowing.
Generosity. Feasting. Prosperous.
And my favorite: **A Father's Help.** Yes.
What a Psalm to combat the orphan spirit.
And to think all year you've been working this birthday Psalm in me.
And now my last month of being 37 I am on this ASK JOURNEY.
No doubt partially due to these verses that I have read and reread not returning empty but accomplishing your purposes Lord.
You truly are a Master Weaver. Such skilled workmanship.
Oh how I need you.
Interesting enough Psalm 38 didn't speak to me when I read it a couple of weeks ago...Papa usually starts speaking to me a good month or month and a half before my next birthday about my next year.
It's all about sickness, sin, and a cry for God to hurry and help.
So I disregarded it and figured another 38 would pop up somewhere else and sure enough, as I have been stuck in Isaiah for quite some time, HS spoke to me there.
Chapter 40 has been huge. Comfort.
So for months I have been in chapter 40 as well as other places.
Oddly enough chapter 40 ends with my eagle verse,

> "Those who wait upon the Lord..."

I usually get stuck on the first half of the chapter so it wasn't until my plaque request came up and out that I put 2 and 2 together and saw it was the ending to chapter 40.
And in this Chapter 40 season HS has led me to go back a couple of chapters to the story of Hezekiah.
Particularly his healing in chapter 38.

Day 22

What I find amazing is, as Brian Simmons teaches, Isaiah is like a mini-Bible. 66 chapters pertaining to the 66 books of the Bible. Now chapter 40 correlates to the start of the New Testament book of Matthew. Making chapters 38 and 39 the last 2 books of the Old Testament. That stands out somehow in all of this, but anyways.

This past Saturday was another session in the Brian Simmons Isaiah study online and it just so happened to be on Hezekiah. Isaiah 38 and 39. I was blown away.
I love your flow HS. I know I've already said that somewhere along this 31-day journey and I'll probably say it again before I'm done. Truly you astonish me.
Connecting the dots and putting puzzle pieces together like those giant kids' activity books with the connect the dots and mazes and matching...
You enjoy what you do-don't you?!
You delight in your role in my life. I can feel it!
The satisfaction you get when I finally get an "aha!" moment!
Like charades or better yet a treasure hunt. Haha!
Child's play.

So ch.38. Isaiah. Hezekiah.
As I was listening to Brian I knew God was confirming this to be a key chapter for my 38th birthday and year.
But it wasn't until last night after reading my yesterday's entry about my sister's healing that I connected the words bitter and healing in chapter 38.
Now theologically speaking this is probably flawed but I don't care. I felt that HS spark last night telling me something is relevant to me in this.
Hezekiah wept bitter tears and then God healed him.
It was almost like the bitterness inside had to come up and out before the healing could happen. And that's the part that feels relevant to my story.
Much like how he had an infected boil...relief comes when the boil bursts and poison, like pus, erupts or is let loose.
IT HAS TO BE RELEASED.
Part of the healing is in letting go of the bitterness.

Father May I?

Once I let go, HS, You can loose its hold on me.

The "tree" healed the Israelites once they looked up.

There is always an action, an exchange.

One can't receive anything, even a free gift, if one's hands are tightly clenched around something else.

Hezekiah released the bitterness in his heart and that allowed God to come and bring healing.

My phone just got my Bible verse of the day text.

> Gal. 6:7 (TPT);
> "Make no mistake about it, God will never be mocked. For what you plant will always be the very thing you harvest."

How very timely. Bitter roots produce bitter fruits.

So Lord I let go and let you uproot all bitterness in my heart.

Like Hez., how he turned his face to the wall, so am I up against a wall.

(The Wilderness of Shur and Jericho both.)

The only wall I need is your SALVATION and I need it to completely wrap around me.

Interesting note.

Hez. received 15 years after his healing.

15 is the number of REST AFTER DELIVERANCE.

2:15 p.m.

So while grocery shopping this morning I escaped to my favorite spot by the river and sat in my van with my Mocha Matcha.

I left the house with my 6-year-old screaming, "Don't leave me!".

Ya, not a great start to the day, I know.

Actually it's been just over a week now of heavy...like pressure in my head and heart both. At first I thought it was just me but when I get headaches day in and day out and less sleep than usual and marital tensions arise and friends are having a hard week too, I start to clue in that a little more might be going on than meets the eye.

As I sat at the river walkway and sipped my lovely soothing hot drink my thoughts turned to Noah as the rain poured down, again, as it has been all week.

Day 22

The Ark was a period of waiting.
They must have gotten restless toward the end.
They must have had "off" days.
As well as the Upper Room.
Acts 1:8 has been so prevalent on my mind as we approach Pentecost and all the meaning #18 has for me.
This Jan-June is a 6-month period that is the end or culmination of an 18-year preparation season. 18 years ago I went to the 1st "Go School" Stacey and Wesley Campbell did in Kelowna, BC in 2002. I am a first fruit.
And at that school I received prophetic words from prophets like Bob Jones, Peter Helms, Patricia King, and many others.
It was a huge seed-planting season.
I then got married and have been through an incredible amount since then. Too much to discuss here but I want to note the importance of 18 to me.
Acts 1:8. Psalm 18. And so many other Scriptures speak of this NEW Era we as the body have just entered. Truly Unprecedented.
I have experienced a reigniting of those 18-year-old words in a way I hardly have words to describe.
One word came to pass on THE EXACT DAY 18 years later. To. The. Day.
Crazy stuff like that, but suffice to say this is my 38th year I am coming up to, as well as my 18th year.
My coming of age spiritually speaking.
The disciples in the Upper Room...waiting...unable to accomplish themselves what needed to happen next.
Same as Noah and his family-all 8 of them, (8=New Beginnings, Restoration, Resurrection.), at the mercy of God's timing.

Both boxed in.
    Up against a wall.
        Much like a quarantine.

As I mulled this over I texted the thought to my mom/sisters chat. Then I opened up to Elijah List on my phone to see the words posted today as I hadn't yet had a chance to browse them like I usually do before breakfast and lo and behold the word I clicked on

Father May I?

by James Goll spoke directly to my current musings. He writes:

> "...Tues, April 3, 2020...I had a vivid dream I was preparing a place of safety for my family and teaching others how to build an 'Ark of His Presence' for the preservation of their families."

He goes on to say how he gave away his blueprint for building the ark and it multiplied and then scores of arks were being built. He then writes about how God gave him these 5 words at the beginning of the year: Repent-Reset-Recalibrate-Recover-Restore. And how we are in the middle of a "50-day Divine Global Reset from Passover to Pentecost"...and writes:

> "...whatever is out of alignment will be challenged. There will be a lot of pulling and stretching as we eventually move into a recovery phase and ultimately, Lord willing, into one of the greatest times in recent history called the 'Restoration of All Things'. (see Acts 3:19-21)"

Then in April he heard the Lord say,

> "I will speak in unusual ways in this season. I have been waiting for such a long time for my people to slow down in order to listen. I have many things to say in these days concerning new ways, new beginnings, fresh alignments and new wine skins for the new wine. I want to share my heart on seed time and harvest-sowing in tears and reaping with joy. Will you turn aside as Moses did?
> I AM there waiting."

He then writes,

> "But revelatory keys for the new era are being released... You simply have to rest around the ark of His covenantal presence and you will receive the new. Ask and you will receive."

Wow. Long but so relevant.
The ark. The upper room. Covid-19.
Seeking your presence above all.
Intimacy over production.
Rest. Abiding. Trust. Safety.

Day 22

Makes me think of #15-rest after deliverance.

I was reminded this morning of Graham Cooke saying to ask Papa what He wants to be for us during this time of quarantine back at the start of Covid-19.
And before I even finished asking the question I heard, "EVERYTHING".

Late afternoon
I just got back from my walk and as I walked I pondered all I wrote down this morning.
Waiting on you.
Becoming more aware of my need for you in EVERYTHING.
I began to sing a song I haven't sang in many years:

> "What a friend I've found closer than a brother
> I have felt Your touch More intimate than lovers.
> Jesus, Jesus, Jesus, friend forever."

And out of my spirit, my deep place, rose a cry that I will call my ask for today, both spiritually and physically speaking.
Simply and profoundly this:

> 1&2) I want to be your friend. God.

And as this cry surfaced and was spoken aloud I experienced a holy hush.
We continued walking as this cry reverberated throughout my being.
Then a strange thing happened as we stood at the boat launch dock on the river.

A dove began to coo.

In all my 13 years here I don't ever remember hearing a dove on my walks. Eagles, ospreys, steller's jays, catbirds, robins, and chickadees yes.
But not a dove.
I looked up and there it was on the power line.
Its coo sounded otherworldly as I felt myself absorb its ethereal sound. The unusual setting made a striking contrast, and I felt all my senses heighten, knowing my friend was speaking.

Father May I?

Yes, you are my Comforter. You are my Helper. You are my Guide.
And you are my Friend.
My Companion.
I am never alone.

As I watched that lone dove I heard "look where he flies" and he immediately lifted off the wire and flew into a very tall, very full tree.

> "Look to the Tree."

You then said to me,

> "Friends talk to each other"

and I knew the pain in my heart had been kept to myself for far too long. You are teaching me to be a friend.
Growing up in the church it has been so difficult to reveal any weakness or struggles without seeming "faithless".
I have learned to stuff it down, creating an opportune environment for the festering wounds of bitterness to exist.
Like the fig poultice on King Hezekiah's boil or the immediate sucking out of snake poison after its bite, it is imperative the poison of bitterness be drawn out of the heart as soon as possible, before it can spread and "defile many".
Talking with you about the hurt, letting you-The Light-see and touch the pain; this is called friendship.
And I have walked lonely, though never alone, for far too long.

> Ex. 33:11 (NKJV);
> "So the Lord spoke to Moses face to face, as a man speaks to his friend."

Let it be so with me.

~May 23rd~ ✷ ~Day 23~ ✷ ~2020~

I have some "gift tags" I want to write down.
1st off I received another $30 from my mom to "get myself a treat"!
Such a thoughtful gesture that really touched my heart, especially this week considering it was not an easy week.
Then we had around $1,000 deposited into our bank account from the gov't for the one-time May payment to help families with kids during Covid-19. Wow.
What a huge blessing and very timely as some expenses have come up and our income is down.
Thank you Papa. I pray you would pour back 100-fold into Mama for her generous heart and action! And I bless our gov't and pray your continued Spirit of Wisdom and Counsel over our PM Trudeau and family and all those involved with governing our country and our province in these strange times.
Also these past few days we have discovered some trends in Hope's blood sugar levels after eating certain foods as well as some helpful online articles, and I'm hopeful that we may have found one of the main causes of her BS instability. I speak with a naturopath in the States who has Type 1 herself this week for some more info, but so far it's looking very promising. We have had periods of success this past week when applying these tools and I remember my prayer awhile back for help with her numbers. So thank you HS. For being our faithful guide and trusted companion. I am feeling confident that together we can manage this with excellence until her full healing is made manifest.
Today we see our dear friends face to face for an evening of cards and wine and fun. It has been months and we are all in dire need of friends and fun.

Father May I?

Firstly I ask you for:

> 1) A most blessed time of refreshing for both them and us. Let there be much laughter, good wine, tasty food, and warmed hearts all the way around this evening I pray.

And my 2nd ask is:

> 2) That you would continue to teach me how to be your friend.

~May 24th~ ★ ~Day 24~ ★ ~2020~

Thank you for a wonderful evening for all!
What a gift to see friends, to laugh, to play, and to hug! We really needed that.
And it's amazing because I ended up having a long chat with my brother on my walk and it was the deepest, most candid 2-hour phone call we've ever had. He was so honest with where he is at and I listened.
I had none of those feelings of having to fix or spiritually advise.
I was just so honoured at hearing the sharing of his heart, all I could do, all I wanted to do, was just be fully present. A witness to his honesty.
Which in turn allowed me to be more real.
I feel you are speaking here in answer to my prayer yesterday about teaching me how to be a friend. It begins with being honest. With yourself and with one another. Wow.
So basic and yet so not easy.
This "connecting" conversation led me to a very honest conversation with my husband. Which was needed to clear the air, much like a good storm in the heat of summer.
This conversation was a bit different than most heart conversations in that I was able to be more honest about the fears behind my reactions and the wounds underneath the current issues.
Honesty. I am becoming more real and less afraid.
The more that is let into the light the less shame and fear have to rule over.
As I ponder this latest insight I think back to the beginning of this 31-day journey. How imperative honesty is in asking.

Father May I?

How can I know my want or need- I mean the REAL want or need- if I'm not honest with myself?
And how can I risk such a vulnerability in my relationships if I am not able to be honest with others?
I think somewhere I have been so afraid of being "wrong" esp. having been raised in the church, by the church.
The dysfunctional legalistic institution of church.
Where authenticity and vulnerability were deadly.
Thank God things are changing.

As I write this I keep seeing the Velveteen Rabbit. "I want to be REAL."
It wasn't being all nice and perfectly put together that made him real.
It was when he was all worn and shabby because of love.
Give me the courage to risk being seen for who I really am and where I'm really at. Isn't that where the journey really begins?
Yes. Today I ask for:

   1&2) Courage. In both realms.

Maybe it won't be scary.
Perhaps it may even be liberating.

~May 25th~ ✱ ~Day 25~ ✱ ~2020~

This whole REAL thing has REALly got me curious.
How have I made it this far?

   And how much farther could I go if I were REAL?
   Real with my questions, the things I am struggling to understand.
   Real with my needs that aren't being met.
   Real with what in our life just isn't congruent with who I am.
   Real about the discrepancies in my marriage.
   Real about how unsafe I feel when my husband drinks (casually never heavily) or how angry I am at not getting out for hikes with friends (when I see hiking posts from friends on FB), when nature is such a huge part of me.

I wonder how much alcohol, food, and screens medicate the places that could begin to heal if only they were revealed.
By honesty. By light. Light in Scripture often equates to TRUTH. The TRUTH will set you free.
(Retyping this out, I just heard it said in a course I am taking that it is "make you free" as Truth is a person who makes us free.)
I always think of that verse in response to Jesus being the Person of Truth.
But in relationships...my relationship with myself even. Yes.
First you revealed bitter roots and now the need for Truth.

It was quite bizarre yesterday as hubby and I sat on the sundeck with a delicious cup of coffee (a rare treat for me!) and were able to be quite "real" with one another, I heard HS say to me as we were wrapping it up to get ready for online church,

   "You are not the enemy."

Father May I?

But HS was saying it through me to my husband and it took me aback.

It was apparent something in me was regarding him in that way just by how that statement hit me.

So we got ready for the day and headed out to the patio table where I set up the laptop and the kids slowly scattered one by one til it was just me and hubby there.

And the sermon opens up with:

> "I want you to turn to the person next to you and say out loud: 'You are not the enemy'"!

I was so surprised; but I shouldn't have been.

This is what you do Papa.

You know how to get my attention and you are very good and faithful to do it.

It was a very timely message about who our real enemy is.

I basically sat there in shock at this simple and seemingly obvious revelation.

Reminds me of how once, not long ago, HS and I were walking and all of a sudden HS told me to forgive so-and-so for hating me.

It was so out of left field I was stunned—much like how I felt during the entire sermon yesterday. Stunned.

So, of course, I did it. I forgave the person. And then, thinking that was rather odd, went back to my enjoyable walk.

Well within days that person turned around and did something so thoughtful for me. I was so blessed and blown away and HS reminded me of that "random" prayer and I knew then there was a connection.

I love how Graham Cooke talks about not letting anyone be his enemy.

Oh, they try, but as long as he calls them friend they can't be enemies.

So then, as the pastor was saying, who is the real enemy?

Again I am in awe, because that is the line in "The Hunger Games" that HS highlighted to me this last weekend as we watched the trilogy with our kids for the first time.

There was one part that really stood out to me when someone says to the main character,

Day 25

"Remember who the real enemy is."

Eph. 6.
A good reminder.

In my email this morning from The Passion Translation:

> "Every trauma can be turned into a place of exorbitant strength when you invite me into your pain."

You came to give us abundant life, to destroy the works of the evil one and to show us the Father.
Help me be real with my pain.
Help me not regard the pain as my enemy.
Or those around me that touch upon that pain. I have a true enemy.
He prowls like a lion.
It's interesting how some predators can smell wounded prey.
Brian Simmons posted about comfort today.

> 2 Cor. 1:3-7 (TPT);
> "All praises belong to the God and Father of our Lord Jesus Christ. For he is the Father of tender mercy and the God of endless comfort. He always comes alongside us to comfort us in every suffering so that we can come alongside those who are in any painful trial. We can bring them this same comfort that God has poured out upon us. And just as we experience the abundance of Christ's own sufferings, even more of God's comfort will cascade upon us through our union with Christ.
>
> "If troubles weigh us down, that just means that we will receive even more comfort to pass on to you for your deliverance! For the comfort pouring into us empowers us to bring comfort to you. And with this comfort upholding you, you can endure victoriously the same suffering that we experience. Now our hope for you is unshakable, because we know that just as you share in our sufferings you will also share in God's comforting strength."

Such a beautiful passage.

FATHER MAY I?

You are the Father of TENDER MERCY and the God of ENDLESS COMFORT.
You always come alongside us to comfort us in every suffering so that we can come alongside those who are in any painful trial.
> "FOR THE COMFORT POURING INTO US EMPOWERS US TO BRING COMFORT TO YOU."

Like Isaiah 40. Comfort my people.
How desperately we have needed the very great comfort of our Father and how massively we have missed it.
What a friend I've found.
I like the NLT of vs 3;
> "God is our merciful Father and THE SOURCE OF ALL comfort." (Capitals mine)

The source.
No other comfort will suffice.
The Berean Study Bible says it like this;
> "...the Father of compassion and the God of all comfort,"

Of course comfort would be the priority of Heaven while we are in this reconstruction transition phase.

Isaiah 40.
   To raise up,
        bring down,
            make straight
                and smooth.
                    Exposing bitterness
                        lies, and disconnect.
                            Comfort is ESSENTIAL.

I don't believe we can receive our healing apart from His comfort.
Everything is about connection.
Everything we encounter and experience is either drawing us closer to Him or creating more distance between us.
I let you love me.
I let your comfort cover and permeate my wounds.
You gently lead.
I love vs. 11 in ch.40

Day 25

Absolutely love.

> "HE WILL CARE FOR YOU as a shepherd tends his flock, gathering the WEAK lambs and taking them in his arms. He carries them close to his heart and gently leads those that have young." (Capitals mine)

Oh and just rediscovered this one...

> Lam. 3:22 (NKJV);
> "...Because His compassions fail not."

Fail not.
So my ask today is:

> 1) Remind me who the enemy is and who the enemy isn't! Let me be quick to love and forgive the people in my life as you continue to expose what needs healing.

Everything I've been through counts for something if it develops compassion in my heart for those who are suffering.
But I am aware that if I myself cannot receive your comfort, your gentle leading, I will not have it to give, so HS I ask that you would:

> 2) Help me receive the overwhelming comfort you have for me.
> Reveal to me your gentle kindness.
> Your tender mercies.
> Your compassion that fails me not.

Amen.

~May 26th~ ✱ ~Day 26~ ✱ ~2020~

Funny. A couple of days ago I sensed a shift.
I thought to myself I bet the calendar is about to change. Sure enough we have entered into a new month in the Hebrew calendar. This is the 2nd time in a row I've felt it and then discovered the why.
So cool. You are getting me tuned in HS. My senses.
Being revived.
Sivan. Began sundown May 23rd. IYAR has ended.
The month of transition is over and we have now entered the month of extravagant PROVISION.
Oh yes Papa!
According to Christine Vales,

> "Provision is supply that has been made in advance for us to use for God's purposes."

And

> "God is the giver of all good things."

Third month. 3 connects to the camel which represents provision.
So awesome.
She also says during her chalkboard teaching on Sivan, 2020:

> "So let's get ready to receive these extravagant gifts from the Lord."

Wow.
Johnny Enlow's post yesterday was all about ASK for the HS. (In Luke)
And today his post was about Christmas in May and HS being like Santa Claus handing out gifts.
The heading is, "CHRISTMAS IN MAY AND EYES THAT SPARKLE."

Father May I?

Even in my sleep-deprived brain-fog state this morning after being at the emergency department til 2 a.m. with my middle daughter who had brutal stomach pain I can feel my spirit tingle with the expectancy of life at those words.

Candice Simmons spoke much of Easter being like Christmas this year with many confirmations. This is such an unprecedented time. And this entire book on asking, on receiving Daddy's good gifts, during the month of May and leading up to the final day Passover. Wow.

Johnny says,

> "He (HS) is shamelessly allowing the connection in thought to our concepts on Santa Claus and His eyes are also sparkling blue. He wants us in child-like receiving mode, as you must become as a little child to receive the Kingdom dimension (Mt 18:3).

> "Everything seems very serious down here, but I tell you, the face I am seeing seems to have not one concern at all—like everything is just fun and games. Of course, if that were true I am sure one of His anointed, Biblical authors would tell us something like, 'In His presence there is FULLNESS of joy.' Oh, that's right, a guy named David did say that in Psalms 16:11. 'In His presence is fullness of joy and at His right hand pleasures forevermore.' Joy and pleasure when you are close to Him? Wow, He must be fun."

Johnny then references Ps. 13:3 (NLT),

> "Turn and answer me, O Lord My God! Restore the SPARKLE to my EYES, or I will die." (Capitals his.)

He remarks here on David's <u>raw honesty</u>.
Honesty. Asking. Crying out.
He then says,

> "The Giver is giving them to us in a very joyful mode and mood. We kill half the power of it all by "the gifts" now becoming too serious of a matter. The rest of 2020 is to be joy unspeakable and full of glory (1 Peter 1:8). GIFTS are to be enjoyed both in receiving and using."

Day 26

Wow. 1 Peter 1:8. Acts 1:8. #18 again.
Before I began this groggy entry this morning, I posted on my FB Heidi Baker's post about being child-like. Standing on Papa's feet. Definitely a theme as we approach Pentecost.
You are restoring to me the love language of GIFTS.
Back to Sivan.
Christine Vales says this month we see a track record of how God gives extravagantly to His children.
Interesting note that the 50-day "counting of the omer" going from barley harvest to wheat harvest has in it provision for the poor as we bring in our harvest and give God the "first fruits". Just like Ruth "gleaned" from another's harvest so are we to leave behind some of God's generous provision-not hoard.
As my kindergarten daughter often reminds me,

   "Sharing is caring."

Generosity must have an open-ended flow.
The vessel must have a receiving place and a pouring out place for what's in it to flow through.
Some interesting "gleanings" from her insightful chalkboard teaching:

- In Exodus 19 & 20 God provides the Torah.
- On the 6th day of Sivan-the 50th day-the 10 Commandments are given.
- Also given Sivan 6 were the plans for the Tabernacle.
- How significant how he foreshadows the coming Messiah's desire to dwell with us.
- And in the New Testament on the very same calendar day another extravagant gift of spiritual provision was given, THE gift: "a mighty wind" and "tongues of fire".
- The gift of the Holy Spirit.

May 29th is Sivan 6 this year.
The actual Pentecost. In 3 days. But Sunday is the Pentecost on our calendar. Either way it's 50 days.

Father May I?

She says to make the blessings in Deut. 29 your own and <u>how gifts need to be received!</u>
And how we need to ASK the Lord <u>how to implement the secrets He revealed to us in the previous month of IYAR!</u> Yes!
I love her monthly chalkboard teachings!
How very interesting we have just crossed over from the transitional month of coming in and receiving secrets as Jesus reveals himself, to the provisional month of receiving the ultimate good gift of HS and going out. (Luke 11:13)
Just as we are beginning to go back out into the world more now that things are starting to open up again.
So Papa, in light of me practicing asking for 31 days I ask you:

> 1) Please pour out your Holy Spirit upon me and my family this Pentecost like nothing we've ever experienced before. Beyond all we can think or imagine.

BLOW RUACH. BLOW OUR MINDS. BLOW OUT THE OLD AND IN THE NEW. BLOW RUACH BLOW.
HS open wide the windows of our hearts and home that you may BLOW IN AND BLOW OUT.
A pouring in and a pouring out.
That we would indeed be blessed to be a blessing!
My 2nd ask is:

> 2) Would you help me find/make time (and energy) to read your word and wait in your presence esp. these next few days leading up to Pentecost.

I feel as though these sleepless interrupted nights are an assassination attempt on my focus and strength as I am so very wrecked during the day lately more than our "usual".
Protect my focus.
Our secret place, I pray.
Amen!

~May 27th~ ✶ ~Day 27~ ✶ ~2020~

I feel pressure adding up.
With each passing day it is harder to get to this journal.
Not only do I feel a physical resistance due to some difficult nights lately, but also a spiritual one.
I will finish this. 31 days.
In your strength Papa. In fullness of Joy.
This morning as I was making my mocha matcha and my kids were hanging around stalling from starting their chores I felt so "yuck."
Tired. Achy. Train-wrecked.
And I had a moment where I made a choice to shake it off and I got real goofy as I blended the almonds for almond milk.
With each blender pulse I began to shake my body until my whole body was convulsing from the blender "shocks".
My 6-year-old laughed hysterically.
Even my 2 teen boys couldn't keep a straight face.
I felt a shift in the room's atmosphere. In my inner atmosphere.
The Kingdom is child's play.
I cannot afford to lose that in this.
Christ's resurrection power in me trumps ALL.
Holy Spirit come. Reignite me.
As Johnny Enlow said,

    "Restore the sparkle".

It's funny how his countdown to Pentecost posts are about God restoring the sparkle in our eyes.
That's a very personal prayer between me and Papa that goes way back. It has long been the cry of my heart.
One of Papa's names for me is "Bright Eyes".

FATHER MAY I?

As I got in the van a couple of days ago it was the song "Total Eclipse of the Heart" but the lines ♪Turn around Bright Eyes♪ and ♪I need you more tonight and I need you more than ever♪ really stood out.

So the book of Ruth is read during the month we just entered- Sivan.

Ruth. My beloved story Ruth. And Boaz.

The 8th book in the Bible. 8. New Beginnings. Restoration.

Comes after 7. Rest. My son Noah; name means comfort and rest.

His brother after him is named Boaz. So I have a Noah and a Boaz.

HS spoke to me at the front end of Covid-19 and told me we are being established in #7 (rest and comfort) in our ARK (as in the days of Noah) and once we were firmly established we would move from that place into the Days of Boaz.

Of knowing Jesus as our Boaz.

Provision. Month of Sivan. Book of Ruth.

I had no idea of this connection when HS spoke that to me but I knew it was time because of the physical confirmation; just this past season my son Boaz has come into his own.

He is thriving. His voice is changing but his kind nature remains. He is shooting up and people are beginning to "see" him.

Even I am seeing him with NEW EYES.

His name means "swift" as well as "strength is within him".

The Lord spoke to me about how once we are firmly established in REST and HIS COMFORT, from that place, there will be a swift move of the Spirit.

Again, when He told me this at the start of the year (in my regular journal) I didn't know we'd be in this season now of going from our quarantined "ARKS" to Pentecost-a swift move of Holy Spirit.

A SWIFT WIND.

Interestingly enough, last night we had big gusts of wind suddenly occur.

Right as I happened to be watching the "A.D." Netflix episode when HS comes upon the disciples as a blowing WIND!

Day 27

In Jesus, our Boaz, we go from gleaning the fields to owning them just as Ruth did. (My pastor and dear friend shared that with me once and it "blew" my mind!)
Another strange observation.
We have a mama bear and 2 cubs hanging around here this past 2 weeks. Right in our yard.
And when we first saw them, so very tiny were the cubs, I felt like I heard "double".
Now I've heard other prophetic voices say 2020 is the year of double.
Double for our shame.
And even Brian Simmons read last Saturday in Isaiah 40:2 (TPT):

> "Prophesy to her that she has received from the hand of Yahweh twice as many blessings as all her sins."

Double.
But I heard it when I saw the twin cubs.
I always need to hear it for me.
Well, Christine Vales said that this month the correlating constellation is Gemini. I didn't realize my birthday falls into this time as I've never been one to go near astrology. Not mistaking it, of course, with astronomy.
When she said Gemini means twins I instantly remembered "double".
How many times have I cried out for a double portion of honour for all of the shame I have known.
As I write this HS is reminding me of the word I received when I inquired of the Lord the first week of lockdown. I knew I had to hear Him; had to find my centre. So much fear was spreading. The stores felt strange and people seemed suspicious. The news was scary.
And your response to my inquiry was FAVOUR.
You told me that Your FAVOUR was the antidote to the fear.
To not try and fight the fear but stand in His FAVOUR.
Like Ruth who found favour with Boaz.
Boaz displayed "hesed": merciful, compassionate loving-kindness.

> Ruth 3:11 (NKJV):
> "And now, my daughter, do not fear. I will do for you all that you request..."

Father May I?

(Or "all you ASK".)

A while back I cried out to you for help with stabilizing Hope's numbers. Yesterday I got a phone call from a new member of our diabetes team we work with and had such a delightfully candid conversation with her as she herself has T1D.
Oh to talk with someone who actually gets it has been so refreshing, so encouraging. The new dosing methods I've been researching online and experimenting with all week she was able to speak into.
Honestly I almost brushed her off. The last thing I wanted to do was talk to another "expert".
I almost missed the gift.
Keep me humble Papa.
Pride is ugly and misses the gifts you so eagerly bestow; like Johnny Enlow's "Santa Claus" laughing with joy as he threw gift after gift.
I see the tag on this gift and I thank you. I praise you.
You are good to me. You see me.
You care about what we are going through.
You not only care but earnestly desire to be an engaged participant.
A Guide. A Giver. A Friend.
Perhaps you don't want us figuring it out on our own.
Maybe this is also about community:
Being a body.
Needing one another.
Losing our independence.
Hmmmm.
Definitely food for thought....finally a true carb-free food! Ha!
And today I have a phone meeting with a T1D naturopathic Dr. from the States.
My first ask for today is:

> 1) That you would make it clear if her member's course is a resource from you that is worth investing in or if her online videos are helpful enough. I ask you to make it OBVIOUS to me.

Day 27

No more wasting time.
As I sang "The Blessing" with my church's worship team live Sunday
I heard a deep cry rise from my deep, calling to your deep.
It was the stanza,

> ♪ May His presence go before you
> And behind you, and beside you
> All around you, and within you
> He is with you, He is with you ♪

Exodus 33:15 (NAS) then ROSE UP within me;

> "Then he said to Him, 'If Your presence does not go WITH
> US, do not lead us up from here.'" (Emphasis mine.)

And I realized I could go forth in this next season out of the ARK
and walk ahead without His Presence.
It brought the Fear of the Lord to me.
Knowing it is possible, that it could happen.
I cannot risk taking even a solitary step without Your Presence.
It's YOU I want.
More than the double blessing.
More than the walls crashing down.
More than owning the fields. You.
I ask that you:

> 2) Increase my sensitivity to your Presence. My awareness.
> Let me walk with you as a friend. Side by side. Hand in
> hand. Heart touching heart.

Thank you HS.
That you care. That you are here now. And that you are coming.

> "Lift up your heads, you gates;
> be lifted up, you ancient doors,
> that the King of glory
> may come in."
> Ps. 24:7 (NIV)

24/7

Oh my goodness. I just checked FB as I went to start lunch.
There is a new Shawn Bolz video in my notifications so I watched

it as they are nice and short.
Oh my!
It's an interview with guest Ryan Lestrange and he tells of how God told him to tell a lady blind in one eye that she would see. This lady has an empty eye socket ok!?
So he waited and watched for her "new eyeball" to come and nothing happened. His brain is telling him that he missed this one and nothing is going to happen.
But then after the prayer she says she can see!
They cover her one eye and she can see out of the socket! WITHOUT AN EYEBALL.
Ryan then says,

> "It was the most mind-blowing miracle I've ever seen in my life."

Why this is hitting me so hard is that when I went outside the day before yesterday I picked up Shelby and looked at her empty eye socket, hopeful there would be a new eye. Alas no new eye yet.
But why this miracle at this time in my news feed?
Like of all the miracles and of all the prayer requests in a lifetime these two just "happen" to intersect right now?
I'm not sure what you're saying HS but you have my attention.
You have my attention.

~May 28th~ ✶ ~Day 28~ ✶ ~2020~

Wow. 28 days already.
I feel as though I've been on an actual journey; all the while being stuck in my own home. How bizarre.
After my phone call with the diabetic naturopath from the States I went for a walk and I asked the Lord how come I didn't have the clarity I asked for?
Although I knew she would be an invaluable resource for us I will admit the $2000 (which is like $3000 CAN) for her 3-month course had me conflicted.
Strangely enough I called my mom while making supper (strange because neither of us are phone people) as she had texted me to see how the phone call had gone. I cut my finger and couldn't really text back so I called her and shared the highlights.
She started speaking to me about Papa's generous spirit and how He gives good gifts, basically what I've been writing about these past 28 days, which she doesn't know.
She then shared how Papa has been showing her how vital it is to move forward with what you have and not just sit back and wait for God to do it all.
It was everything you've been saying to me during quarantine.
What's in your hand?
You do what you can and cry out to Papa when you need your little loaves multiplied.
Our conversation reminded me of what Christine Vales said about this month of Sivan. Every month has an action associated with it and this month is "continuous walking".
I actually had a dream the night before last that I was telling someone that this was the key point in Christine's chalkboard teaching on Sivan.

Father May I?

Well on Elijah List this morning a word was posted all about the gift of faith and what's in your hand and God multiplying.
All about supernatural provision and being free from fear of lack.
The generosity of God and exponential miracles.
It's called, "Exponential Miracles - From now till Pentecost and Beyond!" by Ivan Roman.
Also, just a side note as it often happens:
The verse I wrote yesterday, Psalm 24:7-a verse burning in me this season-was also in a word posted on Elijah List this morning by Alane Haynes titled, "A Gate Has Been Opened - Move Forward in Faith".
I love these confirmations.
Yes I believe a gate has been opened.
All the 444's I've been seeing leading up to this time.
444=open door
So back to God being generous and the giver of good gifts...my conversation on the phone with Mom was my clarity.
As she spoke I could see clearly.
Yes, this is what we've been crying out for. Help. Answers.
How can I have come this far and still see $$$ as an obstacle?
Forgive me Lord.
Well, Mom wrote on our family messenger chat about this incredible opportunity and put a call out for any financial support and by the time I went to bed $950 had been given by my family towards the $3000. That's one-third in one day. Less than a day.
My phone just received my verse of the day text.

> Ps. 55:22 (TPT);
> "So here's what I've learned through it all:
> Leave all your cares and anxieties at the feet of the Lord, and measureless grace will strengthen you."

Oh wow.

Carefree.   Safe.   Taken care of.

   Child's play.   Loved.   Provided for.

Good Father, good gifts.
I belong. I have a family.

Day 28

You are restoring to me all that I have lost.
Even more than restoring–You are My Maker of Dreams.
I am Your Dream Come True.
My heart is overwhelmed by your Goodness.
Your Unending Faithfulness.
You never ever leave my side.
The friend who won't let go.
Thank you Papa. Thank you Jesus. Thank you HS.
Help me keep myself in this love.
It's funny how this prayer request, this ask for clarity, you allowed to be answered through another person.
It isn't the first time in this journey this has happened. I can sense you speaking to me about community.
Like in Acts how they shared all they had and no one was in want.
How you not only desire to meet our every need but how you have ordained for us to be the vessel through which you meet the needs of others.
I feel so needy when my needs are revealed...help me to freely receive that I may freely give.
Your grace will strengthen me to live BOLD and UNAFRAID once I leave all cares and worries at your beautiful feet. Pierced feet. Deserving-of-my-most-expensive-nard-feet.
Just heard my "birthday" song ("Have it All") from turning 36 go through my head:

>♪I want you to have it all.♪

And now I hear you say,

>"Come as you are".

Needs and all. You know our need.
You don't despise our humanity; we are your delight. Your treasure.
Let us have fun today Papa.
That I would live knowing the sky's the limit.
One of today's asks is:

>1) For flowers today. Everyone seems sold out of Petunias and I wanted to put flowers on our sundeck this year.
>For the hummers. For the beauty.
>Please lead me to the flowers...or bring them to me...either way!

Father May I?

And my spiritual ask is (although I think flowers are just as spiritual as anything else!):

> 2) For some good connection for my kids. Whether it be me or friends, online or in person, I can see they are all in need of some connecting. The thought of trying to orchestrate that is daunting...so please HS, just let it flow.

Thank you for your desire to demonstrate your goodness to us, for us, through us.
I love you Oh Lord my strength.
I leave my cares at your feet.
You know our need.
I heard you say on our walk yesterday,

> "I like your book".

Haha! I'm glad! Cuz you're the star!
Hmmm I just heard you say,

> "Because I get to be the Hero".

> Ps. 3:8 (TPT):
> "MY TRUE HERO COMES TO MY RESCUE,
> for the Lord alone is my Savior." (Capitals mine)

My True Hero.
Amen.

~May 29th~ ✶ ~Day 29~ ✶ ~2020~

I had such a great time with Boaz yesterday!
After my journal entry I asked him to help me do a bottle run as well as a garbage run for Grandma and he happily came along.
We then used the money from the bottles to not only get ourselves a treat (hot chocolate and mocha matcha!) but had enough left to buy the next person in line a drink.
My son was surprised but intrigued by the idea.
So fun to be generous and to demonstrate it to your child.
Blessed to be a blessing.
Then we had some extra time before needing to be home for a phone meeting so we walked around town looking at the different sculptures recently put on display for our city's annual "Sculpture Walk".
We had so much fun!
You know how you often "try" to connect with your kid and it just doesn't happen at that level? This did.
It was such a delightful, spontaneous surprise and we both came home with full buckets! (From the kid's book, Have You Filled A Bucket Today?)
That was a very fast answer to prayer, Papa!
Perhaps partly because when the opportunity arose I grabbed it- aware of my request and alert for your provision.
I thank you that this journey is helping open my eyes up to your constant involvement in every moment.
To be continuously aware of Your Presence. Habitation not visitation.
Pentecost, where you came INTO us to make your home.
Today it begins 'til Sunday.

Father May I?

I am thinking I would like to fast, although it is always quite hard on my body.
Please direct me in this. I am leaning toward Saturday sundown to Sunday sundown.

10:48 a.m. Mocha Matcha @ Millennium Park

My phone received my verse of the day text while I was journaling the above earlier this morning, and I haven't been able to shake it.

> Matt. 6:33 (TPT):
> "So above all, constantly chase after the realm of God's kingdom and the righteousness that proceeds from him. Then all these less important things will be given to you abundantly."

It seems so key, so instrumental to this Favour the Bold journey. The whole chapter is relevant. I've already written about the birds. Well lately I can't stop marvelling over the abundance and beauty of all the wildflowers right now! Everywhere I walk and everywhere I drive they are on bold display.

Ch.6-Birds and Wildflowers

It's like, in this global Selah, the birds are louder and the flowers are brighter than ever before.
The 2 very things you referenced in regards to taking care of us.
And then comes ch. 7: Ask, Seek, Knock
Matt. 7:11

> "...HOW MUCH MORE ready is your heavenly Father to give wonderful gifts to those who ask him?" (Emphasis mine)

I look to you-You look after me.
Simple, yes. Easy, not always.
Easier for a child.
The wind is really blowing as I sit here and write.
Come Ruach and BLOW UPON YOUR CHURCH!
In the shower this morning I started humming the song "I'm Yours" by Jason Mraz and it was the chorus I was singing out. And I thought to myself I haven't heard that song in awhile. Well, as I was buying my matcha guess what song comes on the radio? Ha!

Day 29

I am hearing it again as I journal so I looked up the lyrics and it is still the chorus that stands out...

> ♪ But I won't hesitate
> no more, no more.
> It cannot wait,
> I'm yours. ♪

It is drawing my thoughts to the story of Ananias and Sapphira. They just keep coming up lately. First on my walk with my sister over a week ago, then the show "A.D." on Netflix and again last night as I was reading Acts in preparation of Pentecost.
I say I'm yours. I say "Here I am". BUT do I fully mean it?
Am I holding back as they did?
Am I being dishonest about holding back?
This whole real/honesty journey has me asking myself some hard questions; it's not just you Papa.
It is such a sobering story.
One that is difficult to understand having happened in the NT not the OT. Like the song lyrics I want my heart to be all in, fully honest.
Was the problem that they held back or was the problem that they lied about it?
Bill Johnson posted this this morning,

> "God's grace and provision is what enables us to fulfill His call: 'Deal bountifully with your servant that I may live and keep your word.'" Psalm 119:17

You were doing a new thing on the earth, pouring out Your Spirit upon all flesh. Not holding back but being so generous and good to your children.
As Bill Johnson says, it is your GRACE and PROVISION we need and you did not hesitate to give it.
You gave your all.
And the response was the birthing of a community, a family, unlike anything previously experienced before on earth.
The people's overwhelming and unprecedented generosity was in response to your generous gift of the HS.
But 2 within the community weren't willing to respond fully.

Father May I?

They wanted to take all you were offering while still holding back and the result was death.
It could not be so.
To fully receive and partially give does not work in your kingdom.
And it was your kingdom being birthed.
And so it is again. In these latter days you have been preparing the hearts of your people, a 2nd coming of Christ in us the Hope of Glory. Ps. 24:7. The King of Glory comes!
You are purging and pruning those things that would obstruct or prevent the flow of your Spirit.
For our sake.
Somehow A & S chose not to trust you fully while wanting all you had to offer.
This is why the shaking.
You need a people so firmly established in the Goodness and Extravagant Love of God that even the death of their comrades can't shake them.
Oh God, help me be honest with myself and with you HS.
Come, this weekend of Pentecost, of Jubilee, and search my heart and see if there is any offensive or obstructive way in me.
And like in Isaiah 40...

> Raise up, bring down, smooth out
> Make straight my heart
> That you HS can freely flow through me
> That I would be a conduit from Heaven to Earth
> With no hidden agenda, no impure motive
> Nothing held back,
> fully trusting in
> The Goodness of My Daddy

We are up against a wall Papa and only you can do what needs to be done.

"I'm Yours."

You've FULLY given me yourself.
Now deal BOUNTIFULLY with me that I would have the GRACE and PROVISION needed to give you my WHOLE HEART holding nothing back.

Day 29

As I wrote that prayer the wind picked up and gusted through my van's open windows, blowing my hair back, and filling me with the fear (awe) of God.
In this holy moment, how do I ask for anything?
You say it is like Christmas time.
I recall the dream I had the last night of the year 2017 of a bunch of wrapped gifts outside my sliding glass door.
I want all you have for me.
For my sake and for my children and my children's children.
For the sake of this next generation: I want to RUN MY RACE STRONG.
So as you brought that up HS I ask that I would:

1) Open up one or two or all of those gifts you have for me, from my dream. I don't know what they are as they are all wrapped up but I trust I will know once I open them!

Ask #2 today is:

2) NEW LUNGS for my Mom.

She loves you.
You love her.
You are well able and so I put a demand on your willingness.
You came to destroy the works of the enemy.
My Mom's enemy. Satan. Sickness. Shame.
I believe you are Good and I believe you want her WELL-unwrapping your gift of LIFE ABUNDANT and OVERFLOWING!
What a testimony to the world of your GREAT POWER and LOVE, the Restoration of Her Breath.
One TOUCH of Your Garment.
      One WORD from Your Mouth.
            One "ruach" BREATH from Your Spirit to hers.
Done. Finished.
Forget not all His benefits.
Forgiven.
    Healed.
        Redeemed.
           Crowned.

Father May I?

    Satisfied.
      This is WHO YOU ARE.
Oh and there's that generational promise again. In Psalm 103 just like in Isaiah 40:

  "So that your youth is renewed like the eagle's."

It's time.
It's time for the eagles to arise Papa. It's time for your wind to come and blow that we would SOAR.
Funny...Mom told me on the phone day before yesterday that she has been learning Gaelic for fun and that her latest word was the word church and in Gaelic it is Eaglais. Eagle. Hmmmm.
Driving home just now "Sweet Surrender" by Sarah McLachlan came on the radio. That's it isn't it?
You give us EVERYTHING and all we can give you in response is our surrender.
Interestingly enough Johnny Enlow's Last Day Countdown to Pentecost post on FB this morning listed 3 songs for Pentecost. The 3rd one was "I Surrender" by Hillsong and he writes that his favorite line is,

  ♪Like a rushing wind...Lord have your way in me.♪

12:30 p.m. after lunch

Oh my. My youngest daughter just called me into her room where she has a stocking up on her wall full of "presents" for her bear. She made it out of paper and tape while I was shopping.
She doesn't know about all of this Christmas/gifts/Pentecost going on...at least not from any outside source.
Obviously she knows in her spirit.
Interestingly she had 5 gifts inside the stocking. 5 is the number of grace.
Reminds me of Bill Johnson's quote this morning.
She has also been asking both of our good friends that came over for cards last week, as well as Gramma this week, for gifts. And I was thinking wow, ok, her love language is obviously gifts but it's more than that, isn't it? Wow. Just had to add that to this.

Day 29

1:52 p.m. a bit later
So I go outside to watch my daughter ride her bike and on my way out I see Jamie Rohrbaugh has a new FB post and its title catches my eye.
About feeling like you've been put on the shelf.
I read it and had to hold back the tears.
I printed the whole thing as it's easier than writing it all...and I'd have to write it all.
Here it is:

> "Do you feel like you've been left out, or like God has put you on the shelf? If so, the Lord gave me a wonderful encouraging word for you today.
> I had a dream this morning, in which the Lord spoke to me for all those who feel like their lives have been put on hold. Here's the word from the dream:
> You entered a place or season in which you were supposed to be learning.
> You didn't necessarily fit in, but you knew you were supposed to be there. You were surrounded with other students, and Jesus was there to teach you all.
> When you entered the place of learning, you found yourself in the proverbial back of the class. You were out of the way there, but you were okay with that. You felt comfortable in the back.
> But then, before you even got started, life interrupted you. Something you birthed required attention, and you had to step out the back. You could still see and hear everything you were supposed to be learning, but you couldn't participate because you were totally occupied with the life situations that demanded your attention. And this made you really sad.
> If you feel like you've been on the shelf, Father God wants you to know today:
> Despite everything that has happened, it's going to be all right. Do not fear or be afraid. You have still been hearing Jesus teach you. Even though you felt like you weren't part of the class, Father God never forgot you for one moment.

And He has come to seek you out.
He wants you to know that, despite all the water under the bridge, it's going to be okay. He's got you, and He's big and strong and solid—much more so than you are:

- He is strong where you are frail.
- He is calm when you are frustrated.
- He is wise, and He sees the eternal perspective, when you are frustrated.
- He has everything covered when you are capable of nothing.

Papa has not forgotten you.
You've been feeling like you've been put on the shelf. Not because of anything you did; just because of circumstances. Other things simply demanded your attention, and you had to take care of them first because they were your primary responsibilities. But you've still been frustrated.
But beloved, tell Papa all about your frustration.
He wants to hug you; to comfort you; to let you rest upon His solidness when your frailty frustrates you. He has come to hold you and put everything back together as only He can."

Brings me back to Isaiah 40:1-4 (TPT):

Your God says to you:
"Comfort, comfort my people with GENTLE, COMPASSIONATE WORDS.
Speak TENDERLY from the heart to revive those in Jerusalem,
and proclaim that their warfare is over.
Her debt of sin is paid for, and she will not be treated as guilty.
PROPHESY TO HER that she has received from the hand of Yahweh twice as MANY BLESSINGS AS all her sins."
A thunderous voice cries out in the wilderness:
"Prepare the way for Yahweh's arrival!
Make a highway straight through the desert for our God!
Every valley will be raised up, every mountain brought low.

Day 29

The rugged terrain will become level ground
and the rough places a plain."
V.11 "HE WILL CARE FOR YOU as a shepherd tends his flock,
gathering the weak lambs and taking them in his arms.
He carries them close to his heart
and gently leads those that have young."
V.29 "He empowers the feeble and infuses the powerless
with increasing strength"
V.31 "But those who wait for Yahweh's GRACE will
experience DIVINE strength.
They will rise up on soaring wings and fly like eagles,
run THEIR RACE without growing weary,
and walk THROUGH LIFE without giving up."

Yahweh's GRACE.
EAGLES RISING UP.
RUNNING OUR RACE STRONG.
I was given some money from my Mom to buy myself a treat a little while back...I believe I recorded it as another 'cheque in the mail'.
I felt it was for something I wouldn't usually buy. A non-essential. A want rather than a need.
A few days later I see a poster online of a girl running-a really neat design-and the verse in Hebrews 12:1,

> "Let us RUN with PERSEVERANCE the race marked out for us",

and I knew that was what I wanted to buy.
Whatever is hindering NEEDS YOUR COMFORT.
I am going for a walk in a bit.
I will pour out my frustrations from this past season.
Just as I felt I was "launching", right after my return from Israel with Brian and Candice Simmons, we were blindsided by the infirmity called Type 1 Diabetes.
Shelved is an understatement.
It will be 18 months to the day-on my 38th birthday in 2 weeks- that my daughter was diagnosed. There's that 18 again.
Yes. Yes I will let you. Yes. Yes. Yes.

Father May I?

Help me let you be the HERO in my story.
YES=surrender.

Strange...I had just said to my hubby that it is starting to feel like there is a lot of water under the bridge, before reading that word. I can't recall using that phrase before and here it is in the above word.

<u>Blindsided</u>: "To blindside is to launch a surprise attack, especially one that comes from an obstructed or hidden place." (vocabulary.com)

<u>Frustration</u>: "a deception, a disappointment,"" (etymonline.com)
Talk about an access point for a bitter root.

<u>Comfort</u>: "to give strength and hope to, to cheer; to ease the grief or trouble of, to console." (merriam-webster.com) and "to soothe, console, or reassure; bring cheer to" (dictionary.com)

Interestingly in Genesis 18:5 (18 + "grace") Abraham says,

> "And I will fetch a morsel of bread, and comfort ye your hearts; after that ye shall pass on..."

in the KJV but in the NIV it says,

> "Let me get you something to eat, so you can be refreshed and then go on your way..."

...from Late Latin confortare "to strengthen much." (etymonline.com/word/comfort)

Oh my. I just did a google search on the Hebrew word picture for comfort and this came up:

(<u>Comfort My People - Nacham - Bridges for Peace</u>)
> "More specifically, nacham means to "draw the breath forcibly, to pant, to groan." One online author wrote that it's a word picture of a "victim who is under crushing weight that has restricted his lungs and caused him not to be able to catch his breath and is graciously relieved."

(I cannot help but think of George Floyd. The man all over the news who was just crushed to death on May 25th of this week by a police officer kneeling on his upper back/neck area. "I can't breathe" is the hashtag circulating the globe regarding this severe injustice.)

Day 29

The article continues...

> "This picture emphasizes the degree of distress involved in the one needing comfort. It gives us the feeling of how much a comforting word or deed means to one feeling crushed-it helps them breathe again."

Mom. I just asked for new lungs for Mom as she can hardly breathe due to severe COPD.
I must go away now and process.
So much you are revealing.
Much response is required.
Shabbat Shalom.
I don't know why I heard that just now but I did. I suddenly feel led to fast from tonight till tomorrow night.
Over the Sabbath.
Shabbat Shalom.
"May you be restored to wholeness on the blessed Sabbath!"
(www.bradenton.com/living/religion/article34489434.html)

Sabbath.
To Rest.

3:56 p.m after my walk.
Well I know I don't usually post so much in 1 day but here goes.
On my walk I vented. I cried. I hurt. And you listened.
As I sat by the river and let it all out.
On the way back it was like how a good storm clears the air.
In fact, there is a storm warning for tomorrow. Interesting.
Anywho.
Things feel better between you and me Papa.
The wind blew the fragrant lilacs right to me as I listened to a robin sing its bold beautiful song and I realized this must be how it is for you when we release our petitions, our hearts' cries and our worship.
FRAGRANCE AND SONG.
The whole episode reminded me of a sculpture we saw yesterday at city hall that was so profound I had to video it and send it to a dear prophetic friend.

Father May I?

One side of the hologram-like display is a woman's face with her hands covering her mouth.
The other side is her hands off, her mouth uncovered and her laughing unrestricted.
It is titled "Listen" and it is about women being heard today.
I know it represents the church.
The muzzle coming off as all the prophetic words have been about in this time, "2020 The Year of The Mouth-The Year of The Roar".
Me talking with you so candidly was like my hands coming off of my mouth. Yes Papa. It's time.
Release the ROAR of Your Comfort,

> as we remove our own hands,
> our own muzzles,
> and walk in honesty with you as a friend.

Now I had planned on 2 requests a day but I feel led to "Sabbath" from my writing tomorrow.
I need to lay down the mediator of pen and paper and be face to face with you. I've heard it said there is no word for "Presence" in Scripture. It is always "face to face".
So I will use one ask today (from tomorrow) and add the other to Sunday giving tomorrow over fully to FAST and REST.
So my tomorrow's request today is for my Dad.
It is his birthday today, May 29th, and I am going to see him with my Mom and sisters tonight at an appropriately socially-distanced lawn gathering.
As I reflect on my Dad and what to get him for his birthday, besides his beloved pistachios, I feel compelled to ask you for something very specific.
He became my Dad the month before I turned 6 years old and although we've had our ups and downs he has demonstrated such a dedication to reading your word and covering me and my family in prayer constantly and for this I am truly grateful. He has very little in this material world but I know in Heaven he is wealthy, with a filled treasury.
My ask is that:

> 3) On top of his heavenly treasures, he would receive an earthly inheritance from you Papa.

Day 29

I have watched him be so forgiving when wronged and so passionate about your Jewish people. He cashed in his pension to provide for us 4 kids. He's been through bankruptcy and has lost a house all the while treating the elderly at his work with such compassion, going the extra mile and always striving to walk uprightly.
So Papa, bless him.
Let him experience your goodness in the land of the living.
Today is his birthday; bless his generous heart. Bless his heart for your people. I want him to see the Promised Land and taste its fruit.
Do it Papa.
He fathered me the best he could and as my true Father I know you will honour him for taking care of me.
Bless him because you're a good Father.
Blow him away with your Goodness.
Whether an earthly monetary inheritance or a winning lottery ticket (hey you work in mysterious ways-no limits remember!?!) or something my finite mind can't dream up...
Do it! For me Papa. For him.
Amen.

We must be a people who CRY OUT!
Just like there needs to be water on the earth that evaporates and condenses into clouds before the downpour SO WE MUST CRY OUT.
Like Dan McCollam said, in the 31-Day Wisdom Challenge regarding why prophetic people hear God for others but not themselves,
    "It's a lack of crying out".
If my people who are called by my name...CRY OUT...
Take off the muzzle.
Stop trying to be strong.
Know your need.
Unmuzzle yourself.
The Church has not allowed herself to be comforted.
I cannot help but see that the renewed strength that the Isaiah eagle rises in comes from COMFORT.

Father May I?

Ok, last thoughts for today...maybe. As I arrived back at my property from our walk I felt you prompt me to list the good things that have occurred as a result of T1D. Not at all inferring that T1D is good. And because I had released all that pent-up frustration and disappointment from these past 17 ½ months I was able to clearly see what good you have already worked.
Here is my list thus far:

1) The restoration in my marriage of being a team. I did the nighttime shift with babies and toddlers all by myself, not to mention scared or sick kids of all ages. Bitterness def. took root there. This round we have been in this together fully. We each take responsibility alternating nights for monitoring blood sugars and administering food or insulin when needed. I truly feel we are a team for the first time ever.

2) 2019 was the Year of My Breaking. I broke open. It took this (T1D) on top of a daughter dying (2013), a son who went missing (2013), my other daughter almost dying (2010), years of raising 7 kids on top of my own family dysfunction to finally break.
To surrender.
To not be able to go any farther in my own strength.
I am thankful for that.
I know I was one tough nut to crack.
This is better.
I may be broken but now Your Light can shine into all the darkness and do what only Light (Truth) can do. MAKE ME FREE.

3) Compassion. I never would have had a taste of what others dealing with a child's illness are going through without this eye opener. As much as ignorance is bliss even You, the God of the Universe, came in human form to experience our suffering. Compassion is invaluable and cannot be bought, only developed. Through pain. This is undeniably true and it has only come through the suffering I have experienced. Your Word speaks of the compassion you had (have) for the ill. Nothing is wasted if the fruit of compassion is given the ground to grow. And it does; as long as the soil isn't too acidic from bitterness.

~May 31st~ * ~Day 31~ * ~2020~
7:27a.m.

We made it.
Pentecost.
The end of "May" but the beginning of "May I".
I sit here with my hot cup of green tea listening to the downpour.
Yes, downpour on Pentecost.
It started raining as a massive storm came through last night; sheet lightning, thunder, rain.
A perfect storm.
The lyrics,

> ♪Like a mighty storm,
> Stir within my soul
> Lord have Your way
> Lord have Your way in me♪
> ("I Surrender" by Hillsong),

still hanging in the air from when I got down on my knees yesterday midday and cried out to Heaven with that song as well as "Here Now (Madness)" by Hillsong UNITED;

> ♪Spirit breathe
> Like the wind come have your way♪

As I took these 2 lyrics and made them my own and released them to Heaven I heard a rumble. Then another. A mini-storm came through midafternoon. Followed by blue skies and sunshine while we ate supper outside together on the patio. Then as we dove into our family game night "Ticket to Ride" the flashes began, lighting up the entire sky.
Sheet after sheet. Boom after boom. The air electric.

Father May I?

Anticipation high. Desperation great.
Oh how we need you HS.
Come have your way.
I fasted yesterday-the Sabbath-the day of REST.
I don't know why but it felt right and if you knew me you'd know I only fast if and when strongly prompted by the HS.
I haven't the grace for it like others I know.
But oh, to be hungry-FOR YOU.
To be thirsty-FOR YOU.
To be desperate and in need-OF YOU.
As I fell asleep last night my spirit kept saying the verse that I had read earlier in Acts 17:28 put into the first person,

"In you I live, in you I move, in you I have my being."

This storm was so severe for all of the Southern Interior of B.C.
They issued evacuation alerts due to the likelihood of flooding.
Warnings everywhere.
All of the snow, still up high melting quickly and joining forces with rain to cause water levels in all the rivers and streams to rise quickly.
Yesterday morning I stepped out with my tea while all was still quiet and it was warm outside!
Like a summer morning. So strange.
I could feel it in the air then. The garden was dry.
I knew they were forecasting rain but I felt prompted to water it anyway as a prophetic act of releasing vapours from Earth to Heaven to add to the downpour.
Similar to my fast. Vapours.
Joining with other vapours released round the globe.
Crying out for you to have your way.
Laying down paper and pen while fasting yesterday because of this hunger for a face-to-face encounter was met with a response from Heaven.
I came across Johnny and Elizabeth Enlow, Rita Springer, and James Goll LIVE from the day before, the 29th, and I watched the 1st few minutes but didn't feel led to watch it all.
I was aware of staying focused during my fast. No time to waste.

Day 31

I ended up skipping toward the end where he (Johnny Enlow) pulls out the shofar and goes to blow it. His daughter then asks him to list the confirming physical signs in relation to the blowing of the shofar again as some had missed it previously and he responds saying that he will go over them again afterward.
So not knowing any of the "physical" signs I sat there postured, hands raised, eyes lifted as he blew the shofar, at which point I was still waking up and was honestly not "feeling" anything.
But I did it anyway.

Well as that shofar blew tears began to flood my cheeks.
I wasn't sad.; rather something was happening. Inside of me.
Once he finished he then went back over the confirming signs. When he got to the 5th mountain (Out of the 7 Mountains: media, government, education, economy, family, religion and arts/entertainment) he said if anyone has tears streaming down their face it confirms the Mountain of Family.
He said that Papa God had taken one of His tears and put it inside your (my) heart.
That you had received POWER in the Mountain of Family.
HIS COMPASSION. HIS HEART.

Well, of course, I then wept even harder!
After that moment finally passed I looked out my study window and saw that one of our wild tiger lilies in our garden had just opened up.
I had been waiting for them to bloom. 5 flower buds.
And the 1st opened that morning. I knew it was significant.
I went outside and marvelled at its stunning beauty.
There is nothing quite like a wild tiger lily. They always stop me in my tracks.
Well. I googled symbolism of tiger lilies knowing there is more to this and apparently in buddhist cultures as well as other religions it represents COMPASSION. Of course.
I have been on such a journey of going through so much pain and injustice in life-with a growing awareness that it is only these sufferings that are developing a deeper compassion for others who are suffering.

Father May I?

This whole Isaiah 40, comfort/strengthen my people, receiving 1st His comfort once we've released the bitterness...
It all began to come together like a beautiful well-planned mosaic as I stood in our garden staring wondrously at our 1st lily blossom.
The Mountain of Family. The 5th mountain. 5 tiger lilies.
The colour related to the Mountain of Family is orange.
And here we have 5 orange tiger lilies opening up as Papa plants His 'Tear of Compassion' deep in my heart.
I have been crying out for confirmation. Direction. Destiny.
And I kept hearing the verse all day long in Lam.3:22 (NKJV):

> "...His compassions fail not."

Oh the wind is picking up.
Yes Lord.

> ♪ Blow away the darkness
> Chase away the fear in our hearts. ♪
> ("Come Holy Ghost" by Norm Strauss)

I almost feel conflicted here my last day of this journal.
Where to go with today's asks and how to end or cap this journey.
A bit overwhelming. But not in a negative sense.
You have done so much, are doing so much.
I feel as though this month of May I have been much like a flower, slowly unfurling its petals, opening up.
Releasing my scent, inviting pollinators to come and take from me to make themselves something sweet.
I know it isn't an end. It has been more like a 31 day beginning.
I'm going to allow myself a bit more sharing space today.
And perhaps there will be an epilogue as this ripens and ages even in just the immediate days that follow.
Firstly I want to make mention that Elijah List posted Angela Greenig's word this morning titled, "Pentecost 2020: Extreme Outpouring-God, Show Us Your Glory!" and inside she shares 3 GOLD keys-Wisdom keys-to help us draw closer to Father.
It is all based on Ex. 33:13-18. It is the 2nd key that stands out.
Key #2:

"...WE NEED TO <u>SEEK</u> TO TRULY HEAR GOD." (Emphasis hers, underline mine)

Day 31

She then quotes Ex. 33:15,

> "If Your presence does not go with us, do not send us up from here...".

She then states,

> "Moses' intent wasn't God's endorsement, He simply wanted more of God. He didn't want what God would give him, because he recognized that the greatest gift he had was God Himself. He simply wanted to know Him." (Underline mine)

Ex. 33:15 is a cry that has risen from the very depths of me as we've explored together, HS, this journey of learning how to ASK Father.
Father May I.
And learning how to be BOLD. Favour the Bold.
Without you all the blessings and gifts and provision in the world is meaningless.
It's nothingness.
You are the Greatest Gift. My Greatest Gift.
You gave Your Son <u>for</u> me.
You gave Your Heart <u>to</u> me.
And You've set Your Holy Spirit <u>in</u> me.
What a 3-stranded miracle.
My ask (1 of 3 today) is:

> 1) Let me always seek Your Face not Your Hand and all these things will be added.

This is such a key revelation or rather rediscovery during this journey - it deserves to be #1.
The 2nd piece I want to be sure I add is a FB post written by Kathi Pelton in December 2019 regarding the year 2020 titled "<u>By My Spirit" in 2020: A Decade of Rest</u>. It was just reposted and as I read it my spirit leapt within me at the joy of having another voice so accurately depict what I have also been hearing in this season.
I have printed the entire word.

Father May I?

Not only does she quote the late prophet Bob Jones about the years 2020-2029...

> "The 2020's will reveal the 'Rest' of God, to where the Body will come into a place of resting in God, where God will rest in us. And in this rest, the enemy will not be able to do warfare, because we are resting in God and He is resting in us. He will accomplish the things He means to do in a people that is at rest. He has always wanted a people that will come into His rest; there never has been one but rest is on the way"....

but she also adds one of the theme verses that has emerged this month, Isaiah 40:31,

> "But those who HOPE in the LORD..." (capitals mine).

Here is the full word by Kathi Pelton:

> "So he said to me, "This is the word of the LORD to Zerubbabel:
> 'Not by might nor by power, but by my Spirit,' says the LORD Almighty Zechariah 4:6
>
> Each time I see the numbers 2020 I see this verse overlaid upon it. As I have prayed into the decade ahead, there are two of the things that the Lord has highlighted to me:
>
> - The sovereignty of God will be displayed throughout the earth.
> - Resting in His sovereignty will be where victories are won.
>
> As I was praying into these two things the Lord began to highlight an interesting item in the new house that my family moves into across the nation (in the Washington DC region) as a prophetic sign. That "interesting item" is that this house has an elevator!!
>
> What?! No, we are not moving into a mansion but was built as a model home for this community and they put everything that was offered into it. An elevator for the three floor is one of those options.
>
> As I listened to the Lord for the meaning of this elevator I saw Jacob's ladder and felt that there would be an ease

Day 31

about going up to the heavenly places and then an ease in returning with the revelation given. There will be a lot of going up and coming back down beginning in the new year.

This will be the source of keeping us out of constant 'ups and downs' in our souls.

After this I looked, and there before me was a door standing open in heaven. And the voice I had first heard speaking to me like a trumpet said, 'Come up here, and I will show you what must take place after this.' Revelation 4:1 The invitation and the open door is before you! The key to entering in is resting in the sovereignty of God. 'Not by might, not by power but by His Spirit!' Just as I was pondering this 'elevator prophetic sign' Patricia King, who raised me up and mentored me as a prophetic voice, released a word and encounter regarding going up in the ease of an elevator to receive deeper revelation!! This was such a confirmation for me (you can find that word on The Elijah List from 12/30).

As our family prepares to move next week to the Washington DC region (we will be in Virginia) I found myself getting emotionally prepared for a battle. Everyone that we know who has arrived there has had to face great battles. I found myself figuring out all sorts of ways to prepare spiritually, mentally and emotionally. It was like a subconscious preparation. As this was happening the Lord interrupted me. He said, 'Kathi, what are you doing? Do you not know that resting in Me is the key to your victory?'

As He spoke those words I remembered the verse from Zechariah 4:6 and then the phrase that says, 'It takes two to fight' kept going through my mind.

The enemy will try to pull you into "fight mode" because the past decade has been a 'warring decade.' We have become more familiar with the battle than the rest of God. It's what we've known and what we are familiar with but it's time to change our 'default' from battle to rest.

As we have laid down all that we have known to enter into the new we need to know that the key to victory in the next decade is spiritual rest. It is an abiding trust, peace and rest that does not engage in the provocation of the enemy that is designed to pull you out of rest and into war. I don't exactly know what that will look like but I trust that He will teach us. This will not be lethargy or inactivity but rather a spiritual rest in His sovereignty. It's a posture in your spirit that aligns your soul. There will be battles but the battle belongs to the Lord and will be won through the rest of the Lord.

I learned many years ago that supernatural peace was the key to my personal warfare being defeated (which you can read about in my 30 Days to Breakthrough: Stepping into Peace book).

Where there is peace there is no fear or warfare! But this rest will take us deeper and it will be the one thing that the enemy cannot fight. You will be like a warrior of rest.

Then I came across a word by Bob Jones that I had never seen before, it is all about 2020-2029 and rest! Here is that word,

> The 2020's will reveal the 'Rest' of God, to where the Body will come into a place of resting in God, where God will rest in us.
>
> And in this rest, the enemy will not be able to do warfare, because we are resting in God and He is resting in us. He will accomplish the things He means to do in a people that is at rest.
>
> He has always wanted a people that will come into His rest; there never has been one but rest is on the way. (Bob Jones)

Rest is on the way!

'...BUT THOSE WHO HOPE IN THE LORD WILL RENEW THEIR STRENGTH. THEY WILL SOAR ON WINGS LIKE EAGLES; THEY WILL RUN AND NOT GROW WEARY, THEY WILL WALK AND NOT BE FAINT.' Isaiah 40:31

Day 31

Hope and rest will be closely tied together. They walk hand in hand. If rest is the key to victory then hoping in the Lord is the key to rest. Hopelessness will drain and exhaust you and battling in the way you have in the past will merely bring you into a war against hope.

Lay down your weapons of the past decade and pick up the spiritual weapons of the next decade which are rest, hope, trusting in His sovereignty, and accepting the invitation to 'Come up here.'

I hear the 'ding' of the elevator arriving and the doors opening to take you up. You will receive revelation and impartation about true rest for your souls and true spiritual rest. This will bring you much healing from the traumas of battle from the past decade.

The doors are now opening...enter in! Happy New Year!"

Wow. Incredible.

Back to the whole REST and COMFORT theme.
My son's name is Noah.
This quarantine is like the ark and the connection between comfort and strength.
The releasing of bitter roots to the gentle hand of Our Good Gardener, making room for the inpouring of His Comfort and Compassion.
Bringing HEALING. Renewing STRENGTH.
Yes, the New Era will not be fought like the previous one.
This is REST. This is TRUST.

> Absolutely SAFE in His Presence,
> Absolutely SAFE in His Hand,
> Absolutely SAFE with Him.

(A prophetic word I received 18 years ago and is on my wall as a daily reminder. He said Absolutely SAFE 3 times to get my attention—it is obviously very important to know I am SAFE. How can one REST if one is not SAFE?)

> You Cover me. (Your Presence)
> You Carry me. (Your Hand)
> You Care for me. (Your Heart)

Father May I?

Isaiah 40. Comfort, comfort my people...
Noah means REST, COMFORT.
The New Beginning after the flood.
A symbolic "New Era" of REST and COMFORT.
And from this place of Restful Abiding our Boaz swiftly comes.
My son after Noah is named Boaz. Born so fast. My only quick delivery; the rest were long and laborious. Not him. He literally popped out. We named him Boaz (swift/strength is within him) Quinn (wise) Quinton (5th born). Swift, wise, #5 for short!
As I write this, completely unplanned on my part, I see the incredibly prophetic picture.
Of how, after REST and COMFORT (Noah) are established the Provision of Grace (Boaz represented as Ruth's PROVIDER and REDEEMER. Boaz is our 5th born child-the # of GRACE) comes SWIFTLY (Boaz meaning swift).
There have been so many words about the SWIFT move of God upon this year-seriously too many to count-I lost track, once I grasped what You were saying.
Our 6th born, Roja Rayne, means Morning Star and Queen which hardly needs deciphering and could very well be the theme of another book perhaps...
I'm in awe.
As the ink from my pen flows on the paper I see Your Handiwork unveiled in my life and all I can do is worship.
I praise you Jesus. I bless you Papa. I love you HS.
You wrap around me as my shield, my Walls of Salvation and surely my gates are PRAISE.
You and you alone deserve all the glory, all the honour, the bowing of every knee.
Here I will pause, selah, before writing my final thoughts.
Blessed be the name of the Lord who is worthy to be praised.
I lay down my journal to go and join my hubby make breakfast with this song on my lips:

> ♪I will call upon the Lord who is worthy to be praised
> So shall I be saved from my enemies.
> The Lord liveth and blessed be the rock
> And let the God of my salvation be exalted♪
> ("I Will Call Upon The Lord" by Petra)

Day 31

3:05p.m.
And it continues to rain.
Potential "historic flooding" today.
Our road is closed for the first time I can ever remember due to a creek overflowing.
Before I begin my next "last day" entry I want to make mention of how I not only found flowers for my beautiful ceramic planters yesterday but also sugar baby watermelon starters that should trail down my planters and grow nicely on my sundeck.
Not only was my prayer for flowers answered but my son, Bo, has been asking all spring for us to plant watermelons and there just wasn't space in the garden. But because of my delay in getting flowers (I usually have them long before now) Bo's request was also granted.
2 asks with 1 answer.
God you're so good.
I had asked for petunias as that's all I have ever done in these planters but I am excited for the chance to branch out and try some new flowers and, of course, the sugar babies!
Thank you Papa. You not only heard me but you heard my son which doubly blesses my heart. Good Gift Giver you are indeed!
I am taking communion as I write this. I am not sure why and why would I even need a why for that matter.
Why not I say.
Or because I can.
At the sound of Heaven releasing its downpour I find myself compelled to commune with you.

We tuned into church online again today.
The Pastor's message was, "Desiring Pentecost" and you spoke to me as you almost always do.
She spoke about the coming of Holy Spirit being all about "DAY TO DAY COMFORT".
That really resonated. Of course.
There's a reason one of HS's names is Comforter.
But we can get too familiar or desensitized to such things over the years, can't we?
It makes perfect sense we would need continuous comfort as we

encounter all that life brings our way.
I love how she told how in Acts 1:4 they were instructed to,

"...wait for the GIFT my Father PROMISED." (Capitals mine)

What a perfect verse on the last day of this 31-day journal about asking and receiving "Good Gifts" from Papa.
Wow. I am still in awe of the timing of Pentecost and the end of this book.
Where all could receive the GIFT of CONTINUOUS COMFORT.

Another bizzarity (a new word-you heard it here first) is the prophetic word I stumbled across, I don't even know how, from Jan. 2, 2020 by a man named Kent Christmas.
Yes, that's right. CHRISTMAS.
I knew I had to listen although a total stranger to me.
It was titled, "The Rain of Favor". Well you had me at hello! Like really!
The word God gave me going into quarantine was FAVOUR.
And here at the end of 31 days we are experiencing a massive "historic flooding" downpour Pentecost Sunday. Haha!
And if those 2 things (Christmas and Rain of Favor) aren't enough these 2 things he said require mention, I feel:

> 1) For all my children who have sown in tears will reap in joy. The next generation will be led by a people with a Joshua and Caleb spirit. They spent many years in the wilderness <u>but they did not become bitter</u> waiting on me to show up. I have preserved their call and purpose for this time." (Underline mine)

And that 2020 would be the beginning of the "Fullness of the Glory of God":

> 2) "I have a remnant of people who have been broken and I can trust them because they will not promote themselves. I am going to GIVE YOU, says the Lord, MORE THAN YOU ASKED FOR starting in 2020." (Capitals mine)

From a man called "Christmas". Too good not to mention. Yes Papa. As the pastor preached on having a desire to hear God and to press in I kept mulling the sermon title in my spirit.

Day 31

Desiring. Hungry. Asking. Crying out. Seeking.
And my 2nd request in the form of Scripture came forth.
Request numero dos, Ps. 37:4 (NKJV),

> "Delight yourself also in the Lord,
> And He shall give you the desires of your heart."

Now here my ask is two-fold.
I know this verse likely means you will give me what I most desire and yes, you know my deepest desires are
TO SEE MY ENTIRE FAMILY OVERCOME WITH PASSION FOR YOU, TO SEE THE WORLD AND TO **RUN** THE **RACE** YOU'VE MARKED OUT FOR ME, NOT MISSING ANYTHING, BUT FULLY ACCOMPLISHING ALL YOU'VE CALLED ME TO DO (and deep breath in! That was a mouthful!)
And of course I ask for those desires. Please Papa.
But the other possible interpretation is my main petition in this moment:

> 2) Give me Your desires. Place Your Desires in my heart like you placed your tear there yesterday @ the blowing of the shofar.
> That Your Desires would become My Desires.
> That I would want what You want.
> Like Father, like daughter.

It's here I want to insert what I posted on FB this morning when a picture memory popped up from 2 years ago: "When I see a memory pic like this one from 2 years ago my first thought is "Is that a pre-diabetes diagnosis or post-diabetes diagnosis picture?" It's amazing how certain moments can be so defining. We never know what's ahead... How quickly our lives can be turned upside down. We encountered another such defining moment 7 years ago that changed our lives forever. Anyone else who has been marked by tragedy knows this truth. But as we step into this New Era I sense a compelling invitation to lay down my personal timeline and allow His Divine and Eternal timeline to overlay and overlap. And as I see this in my mind's eye I see mine dissolve into His. Like it is absorbed into. Not erased. But changed. Metamorphosized. Even our calendar system boasts this truth. This greater reality that overcomes our known reality: B.C. and A.D.

Father May I?

Today is Pentecost.
The day the disciples were able to personally receive the empowerment of what was finished at the cross and what was begun in the empty tomb.
The POWER of Christ's Divine and Eternal Timeline written in their hearts forever.
Acts 1:8 POWER
And Acts 17:27 the verse burning in me as I fell asleep last night to the sound of thunder and the flash of lightning filling my room, my heart.
"In Him I live, in Him I move, in Him I have my being."
This thunderous voice crying out from this wilderness "Prepare the way for Yahweh's arrival".
For the overlay of His Timeline upon Ours.
Let this be THE defining moment in our lives, in my life. Where every hurt and trauma and attack must yield to the Empowerment of Christ in me, the Person of Truth that conquers every lesser reality.
Let us make way for Christ to be our one continuous Defining Moment.
Let it be so.
Because of His compassions that fail not the bitter poison, the traumatic moments, they can be comforted and healed and therefore no longer allowed to define us.
I have greatly underestimated the power of God's compassion.
All the prophetic voices announcing the coming of His Glory (Ps. 24:7) make me think of Moses and God causing all His Goodness to pass by.
I don't know what all this "goodness" entails, but could it be that this next and possible final move of God on the Earth is birthed in Compassion and Comfort?
The 1st time Jesus came it was not as expected. Quite the contrary.
What will this next move of God look like? I don't know.
But just as Noah, during the time of global flood waters, stepped out and into A New Beginning so too are we, I sense, crossing over this Pentecost into The Great Unknown.
Who is this King of Glory?

Day 31

And last but not least, #3.
Yesterday sundown ended Shavuot.
The holiday of the giving of the Torah.
The day 2 loaves of leavened bread were offered up to God representing a first-fruit offering of the wheat harvest.
Pentecost is the "eighth day" of Passover.
7 weeks of counting the omer, the Feast of Weeks, which is 7 days x 7 weeks=49 days and then the day after, the 50th day is Pentecost.
Pentecost means 50.
The "8th" day of the week.
I found this at <u>What Are the Two Loaves Presented on Pentecost?</u> (hope-of-israel.org):
Lev.23:15-17 (Ferrar Fenton Version);

> "You shall also count for yourselves from the day after the Sabbath that you bring the Wave-sheaf, seven Sabbaths. They must be complete. Then after the seventh Sabbath, you shall count fifty days, when you shall present a NEW OFFERING TO THE EVER-LIVING. You shall bring from your dwellings two wave cakes of two tenths of fine flour. They shall be fermented—baked in an oven for the EVER-LIVING." (Capitals mine)

And I quote,

> "Notice! Leaven is compared to the holy spirit, which is put within YEHOVAH's people Israel, and changes their corrupt human nature into the wonderful, holy, righteous nature of the holy spirit, the Spirit of YEHOVAH God -- the nature of YEHOVAH God (II Peter 1:4)."

The above site speaks of how directly following Passover the first fruit of the barley harvest was a sheaf of barley (The Feast of Unleavened Bread) and then 50 days later the first fruit of the wheat harvest, the 2nd harvest, were the twin loaves of leavened wheat bread (Shavuot).

And how the 1st "FIRST FRUITS" OFFERING REPRESENTS JESUS AND THE 2ND "FIRST FRUITS" OFFERING REPRESENTS US, THE BRIDE.

Father May I?

And the story of Boaz and Ruth is read during Pentecost which is a picture of Christ and His Bride.
Fascinating.
Twin loaves. Leavened. Filled with Holy Spirit.
Gemini, the Twins, is the constellation that correlates with this Hebrew month of Sivan according to Christine Vales. (My birthday falls in this time-frame as well.)
We keep having that mama bear and her 2 cubs show up.
All of this drawing my attention to the words first fruits and double.
This is all leading up to my 3rd and final ask Papa.
(At least for this 31-Day Journey. It's really just the beginning.)
Of living in a posture of CONFIDENT EXPECTATION You Give Good Gifts and love to meet my needs.
Even yesterday when another need arose and my husband sighed, I said to him,

"No, I do that too but let's not. Let's be glad 'cuz needs mean we're alive. As long as we're living we'll have needs and same with those around us. Let's stop seeing our needs as bad. Instead let's rejoice that Papa already knows our need. There is nothing we come up against He hasn't only seen but has also provided for somehow someway. And the joy is we get to journey it together. Fully assured He's a Good Papa."

OK, back to first fruits.
Lev. 23:9-10 and Prov. 3:9 speak of first fruits:

> "When you come into the land which I gave you, and reap its harvest, then you shall bring a sheaf of the first fruits of your harvest to the priest" (Leviticus 23:9-10)

> "Honor the Lord with your substance (wealth), with the first fruits of all your increase" (Proverbs 3:9)

First fruit in Hebrew is "bikkurim" and literally means "promise to come." As Paula White writes,

> "When you keep First Things First through faith and obedience, you turn GOD'S PROMISE INTO PROVISION... This divine establishment of God's order is actually the root, the foundation that governs the rest. "For if the firstfruit

Day 31

is holy, the lump is also holy; and if the root is holy, so are the branches" (Romans 11:16 NKJV).

And,

"God claims the FIRST of ALL THINGS! It rightfully belongs to Him... It is a principle...Jesus declared, 'But seek first His kingdom and His righteousness...all these things will be added to you,' (Matthew 6:33). God adds the 'things' to you when the foundation is in place to be built upon."

There is a law here.
I love the 1st line and I think it is a key point in this asking journey.
I ask you Papa to receive this, My First Book, as my First Fruit offering.
It is for you.
I don't even know what that looks like but I trust you Holy Spirit to lead me in it.
You called me to write a book.
It was by divine inspiration, I believe, that I was compelled to write a book titled Father May I in my own personal journal style. 31 days.
You even surprised me with the Greatest Gift on the last day.
Pentecost. 50. Jubilee.
The freedom and joy that comes with the receiving of HS.

I don't know if this book will be between you and me or if it will be shared. All I know is it's my 1st and it's yours.
Papa it's all yours. I am all yours.
    Thank you for this journey together.
      You are My Song and My Delight.
        I feel the door of the ARK opening.
          Here we are.
            Let's do it together.

Into the New & Great Unknown.

~EPILOGUE~

June 1st
Life now can truly begin.
After Day 50.
The 8th Day.
New Beginnings.
The sun is shining this morning.
The rain is finally over.
The birds are singing BOLD and FREE.
Let us plant vineyards and drink the new wine.
It is June. A new month.
But it feels different.
Like the air after a storm.
Sivan-the month to go out.
I am already hearing you speak such wondrous words about June.
A future filled with such promise.
Behold You make ALL things new.
As I spend the next couple of days going through this book and rewriting out all my requests and documenting the answers thus far the verse that best wraps up this journey, and by wraps up I mean wraps around, is John 14:18 (18 again!) and it says,

> "I will not leave you as orphans; I will come to you." (NIV)

He says this in the middle of the chapter titled "Jesus Promises the Holy Spirit". TPT says it this way:

> "I promise that I will never leave you helpless or abandon you as orphans-I will come back to you!"

June 2nd early morning

I love to end this book by coming full circle.
My journey into asking became an unveiling of an orphan mindset and finally led to the Greatest Gift: Holy Spirit.
In fact all of chapter 14 in John is relevant.
Chapter 14 is titled, "Jesus Comforts His Disciples".
Vs. 13;

> "And I will do whatever you ask in my name, so that the Father may be glorified in the Son."

Vs. 14;

> "You may ask me for anything in my name, and I will do it."

Vs. 16 & 17;

> "And I will ask the Father, and he will give you another advocate to help you and be with you forever- the Spirit of truth."

Vs. 18;

> " I will not leave you as orphans; I will come to you."

And John 15:7 just texted to my phone as the grand finale,

> "If you remain in me and my words remain in you, ASK WHATEVER YOU WISH, and it will be done for you."
> (Ch. 14 & 15: NIV-Capitals mine)

I awoke at 3:33 this morning and I knew it was Jer. 33:3:

> "CALL TO ME, and I WILL ANSWER YOU,
> and show you great and mighty things, which you do not know." (NKJV-Capitals mine)

From here forward let it never be said of me that there was a lack of crying out.

> I call to you
> I cry out to you
> I ask of you
> I ask in Your name
>
> I am unmuzzled.

Epilogue

Day 1
1) fresh God encounter
2) Shelby's eye restored

Day 2
1) look to you-first response
2) cause all 12 sunflower plants to grow

Day 3
1 & 2) "cheques" with my name on it

Day 4
1) birth creativity
2) thank you for word

Day 5
1) speak a phrase/word into my heart-identity
2) Gran's plaque

Day 6
1) put a tag on each gift
2) restore the delight of receiving gifts

Day 7
1) Father-daughter talk
2) increase awareness of gifts/blessings received

Day 8
1) full healing in family in area of diabetes
2) reveal areas you are/want to be Jehovah-Rapha

Day 9
1 & 2) Physical and spiritual bitters made sweet

Day 10
1) confidence and boldness in parenting
(both physical and spiritual children)

Day 11
1) increase hunger for your word
2) 13 lbs by the 13th

Father May I?

Day 12
1&2) a dream

Day 13
1) help me identify limiting thoughts
2) new clothes for my kids

Day 14
1&2) to live from the place of ABSOLUTELY SAFE

Day 15
1) sleep/rest and steady #'s for Hope through the night
2) reveal any areas I need to surrender in

Day 16 ~Selah~

Day 17
1&2) the healing of relational boundaries

Day 18
1&2) Fun! Double the fun!

Day 19
1&2) reveal one step I can take towards "our dream"

Day 20
1&2) remove that which hinders me from running my race

Day 21
1) posturing for healing from bitterness as Pentecost nears
2) bring someone into my path I can bless

Day 22
1&2) I want to be your friend God.

Day 23
1) continue to teach me how to be your friend
2) a time of refreshing as we visit with our friends

Day 24
1&2) courage in both realms

Epilogue

Day 25
1) remind me who the enemy is that I'd be quick to forgive
2) help me receive Your overwhelming comfort that I would be full of compassion for others

Day 26
1) pour out Holy Spirit upon me and my family this Pentecost
2) time/energy to read Your word and wait in Your Presence in the days leading up to Pentecost.

Day 27
1) increase my sensitivity and awareness to Your Presence
2) make it clear if this Dr is a resource from You

Day 28
1) relational connecting for my kids
2) flowers for my deck planters

Day 29
1) that I would open the gifts you have for me (my dream)
2) new lungs for my Mom
3) an earthly inheritance for my Dad (ask 1 from Day 30)

Day 30 ~Selah~

Day 31
1) let me always seek Your Face and not Your Hand (ask 2 from Day 30)
2) place Your desires in my heart
3) that You Papa receive this book as my First Fruit Offering

Notes of some of the answers I received to the above asks:

So much of what I asked for (healing from bitterness, hunger for Your word -both written and spoken, confronting limiting thoughts, knowing I'm safe, becoming Your Friend, receiving Your Comfort, increased awareness of Your Presence, areas I needed to surrender and the grace to do so which led to giving up caffeine, sugar, and alcohol for this season so I would have no crutches

Father May I?

to impede my healing, confidence in parenting, healing in area of relational boundaries, having fun, taking hold of the gifts you have for me, discovering Your desires in my heart and most obviously learning how to "ask") have all been ongoing and increasing over these past 10 months since I completed My 31-Day Journey. I would have to say this is especially true for Papa faithfully exposing bitter wounds and healing them through my discovering His Comfort and Compassion and through me learning how to "pray continuously" by keeping a flow of dialogue and open connection with HS regarding even all the "delightful details" (Ps.37:23 NLT).

I did journal throughout some of the specific answers and have a few more to add:

<u>Day 2</u>) Cause all 12 sunflowers to grow.
Well You answered that request in a very strange way. Go figure. So long story short only 7 grew and of those 7 one head broke off right as it was maturing and filling with seeds, one was delayed and was barely half the size of the rest when we harvested but had a little head that was rapidly filling with seeds, the other 5 grew big and strong and filled beautifully with much seed, and of those 5 one shot up a head above the rest. Now it isn't too often my hubby and I hear the same thing so clear but this was one of those times. We both knew those 7 sunflowers represented our 7 children. The one that broke just entering maturity rep. our eldest daughter, who died in a car accident at 18 years old. The half-sized one that found itself more challenged than the others but wasn't held back from filling with seed rep. our youngest daughter who I have written about in this journal regarding T1D. (The caboose-just 6 years old in May 2020.) The other 5 rep. our other strong and healthy children filled with seed that we enjoyed the fruit of all winter long, which speaks to me of our assurance that Your Word is planted deep within their hearts and they are growing and becoming fruitful. The one that shot up above them all rep. our youngest son, Boaz, who has not only shot up in height this past May and these past 10 months but as I write in the book HS is highlighting "Boaz" in this season. As One who Protects, Covers, and Redeems. So HS did it His Way with the sunflowers and I'm so glad!

Epilogue

What a powerful visual it was for both my husband and me and an opportunity to connect on hearing Papa speaking to us both.

<u>Day 11</u>) 13 pounds by the 13th.
Haha, this one is hilarious. I gained weight leading up to my birthday not lost it! But that is a whole other journey in itself in regards to foods and diet and gut health. Suffice to say I did lose all that extra weight this past fall and winter and have been holding steady. So thank you Papa for that! Better late than never!!

<u>Day 12</u>) A dream.
I have had many. I mean I know this one was answered immediately in the book but since then I have had numerous powerful and revelatory dreams that have been key in my healing and wholeness journey. And may they continue! Thanks HS.

<u>Day 13</u>) Clothing for my kids.
I honestly started to put this request in the "haven't seen an answer yet" list but then realized it has been answered just not in the way I had pictured. We were never able to go to the nearest big city to us and hit Value Village and buy clothes for my kids like we do every Spring Break. But throughout the past 10 months my kids have recycled their old wardrobe, and been given the odd and very timely pair of pants here and there from friends. We managed to score a couple of items at local stores and one of my teenagers got a job and bought a bunch of clothes online. It worked out. Wowsers. Who woulda thunk it?!?
Thank you Papa.

<u>Day 28</u>) Relational connecting for my kids.
With this one it definitely got worse before it got better but it did get better. Way better. I have been in awe this past 2 months at the healing and development. I can see the beginning buds of Restoration in my family. Thank you Jesus.

And then there are those I know are answered but have not yet fully manifested for reasons I know not, but this I do know: I TRUST You.

Father May I?

<u>Day 8</u>) Full healing in family in area of diabetes.
This one is huge obviously. A journey all in itself. I don't know what I don't know but what I DO know is this assassination attempt from the enemy has been the catalyst that Papa allowed to Break Me Open, thus beginning the true healing journey of our family and the dysfunction of my family line. I SEE Life, I FEEL Your Comfort and Compassion and I am EXPERIENCING "Hope for the Future".

<u>Day 29</u>) New lungs for my Mom.
Again, this is one I am beginning to SEE and remain expectant that My Mom will "see the goodness of the Lord in the land of the living"!!

These ones I am still waiting for Your Response Papa...Your Timing.

<u>Day 15</u>) Sleep/rest and steady #'s for Hope through the night.
I am resting more at night these past 2 months than I have since this began-Thank you Jesus-but am still needing more sleep than I am getting.

But I have also had to learn to rest in the day. To slow down. It became not optional. Which forced me to slow everything right down during this Covid time which has been crucial to my wholeness journey. A stellar example of Papa causing something that was fashioned to harm me to benefit me. This is who you are.

<u>Day 29</u>) Dad's earthly inheritance.
Like I said above-in your timing. And perhaps this one is personal between You and Dad. Still expectant.

What else can I say regarding the answers to all my asks.
Each response as varied as every request.
It has become easier to ask.

When finances come up HS whispers to me and I repeat it aloud,

"My Papa foots the bill."

When emotional pressure builds, or even before it gets a chance, I remind myself of how much you care for me.

Epilogue

Everyday and all the day long
You are the Father who helps me,
who knows my need before I even ask
-My Hero.

Father May I?

Passover:2021 03.28.21

I just finished typing out my book. 10 months later.
Turns out 10 months is a full-term pregnancy for humans Dr's are now saying instead of 9 months (according to today.com).
Birds are singing.
I woke up anticipantly expectant about reading Ps. 118.
(I have been reading a Psalm a day for 118 days to be precise just as a personal daily practice. What completely got me though was how as I neared finishing typing out my book last week I noticed a footnote on Psalm 113 in TPT that said Psalm 113-118 were sung during the Jewish Passover celebration.
Then yesterday I realized as I read Psalm 117 that I would be reading the last Passover Psalm (118) today, Passover 2021, as I type out the last few pages of my book. I finished my book on Pentecost 2020 and finally completed typing it out on Passover 2021.
That's like "back to the beginning". Not a coincidence.)
I have been slowly retyping it all winter 30 minutes a day.
It is the month of Nisan.
The month of New Beginnings.
A New Spiritual Year.
It is a Miracle Month.
The Month of Spring.
   "See! The winter is past."
I don't know how to wrap up the book...in response to all the asks... as I have my breakfast and read Your Word please direct my heart and my hand HS!

As I begin to read Psalm 118 my dearest friend Marg sends me a timely picture via FB messenger of a woman on a white/gray horse, her head uplifted with joyous countenance, her arms spread wide and leaning back slightly holding a white and gold banner.
A red skirt and red horse gear. She is in silver armor. It is beautiful. (You can view it at https://www.deviantart.com/dani-lachuk/art/The-Exhaltation-of-Joan-of-Arc-348396763)
Her face. Her expression.
Weightless and Carefree. Joy uncontainable. Free.

Passover 2021

This is what she said with the pic,
> "Made me think of you as soon as I saw it.
> Happy Sunday to you! Wear your righteousness like an armor of Innocence."

On Passover!
Makes me think of "Return to Innocence" by Enigma. A song I listened to over and over in my dreaming teenage years:

> "Don't be afraid to be weak
> Don't be too proud to be strong
> Just look into your heart, my friend
> That will be the return to yourself
> The return to innocence"

I just googled the lyric video. 4 years ago. 4.4k likes. 444.
Back to Psalm 118.
I am struck by vs. 17 (NIV) as it is a life verse for me and my generational line-both up and down;

> "I will not die but live, and will proclaim what the Lord has done."

And vs.19 (TPT):

> "Swing wide, you gates of righteousness, and let me pass through, and I will enter into God's presence to worship only him."

(Just like the women in the picture's arms are flung wide!)
Sandwiched in between those 2 incredible life verses of mine...vs.18 (CJB);

> "Yah disciplined me severely, but did not hand me over to death."

18 years. Psalm 118
So in order:

1) I will NOT die BUT LIVE and TELL of all you have done for me
2) You have DISCIPLINED me severely (A Father disciplines a child in whom He delights-Prov 3:12)
3) So SWING WIDE, you gates of RIGHTEOUSNESS, and let me pass through.

"I have found the gateway to God." (vs.20 TPT)

Father May I?

444 Open Door
His name is Jesus.
My Righteousness.
My One Defense.
My Return to Innocence.

This Pass "Over" I will Pass "Through." Back to vs.5 -the # of GRACE,

> "Out of my deep anguish and pain I prayed,
> and God, you helped me as a father.
> You came to my rescue and broke open the way
> into a beautiful and broad place."

Jesus. You gave Jesus.
As my Papa You gave the Darling of Heaven to answer my prayers, my asks, which are all but one cry really To Come Back To You.
And Your Response BROKE OPEN THE WAY BACK.
Swing wide for me the Gates of Righteousness...
I'm coming through.
I'm coming UP.
Come Up Here.
444 Jesus The Open Door.

> The Heavens Rent
> The Veil Torn
> The Father's Response
> The Son's Surrender
> The Holy Spirit's Great Love and Comfort...
> And guidance back...
> Always back to the beginning
> And UPWARDS

UPWARDS-IN CHRIST AND CHRIST IN ME,
THROUGH CHRIST, "The Gateway to God",
I find You. Father.
Were there all along.
I look back and see You NEVER ONCE left me.
And I rediscover Skye.
I am the Darling of Heaven,
and the Apple of Your Eye.

Your Beloved Child.
And I look just like You.
Like Father, like Daughter.
So I RUN INTO YOUR ABUNDANCE (Phil 3:12 TPT).
I RUN into Papa's arms.
Psalm 118:7 (#7=completion)

> "For you stand beside me as my hero who rescues me.
> I've seen with my own eyes the defeat of my enemies.
> I've triumphed over them all!"

And vs.8-our new beginning-begins when we,

> "Take REFUGE in the Lord." (Capitals mine.)

Trusting only in Him, not in one another or our own strength, not in humanness, ourselves.
REFUGE=Hebrew root word "chasah"
According to WORD STUDY-HE IS MY REFUGE
www.chaimbentorah.com,

> "Ancient Semitic man when they heard the word chasah did not just think of refuge, but of atonement as well."

And,

> "Chasah which means a shelter, protection, or to go aside. It is the same word that is used for a city of refuge. It is also a word used for trust...the idea of a confidence or a feeling of security in something or someone."

Reading the article we see that the cities of refuge were not a place of refuge but of ATONEMENT.
The fugitive went through a process of atonement in said cities of refuge.
If the killing was premeditated, then the fugitive was turned over to the relatives of the deceased to do with the fugitive what they wanted.
If it was deemed accidental the fugitive was fully atoned for and allowed to go free with the guarantee of not being harmed.
The key point here (for me) is this:

Father May I?

> "...according to the Talmud, if the high priest should die all the people seeking asylum for having killed someone who was living in a city of refuge would automatically receive atonement for their crime. The death of the high priest would atone for their crime. Upon the death of the high priest all were free to leave the city of refuge unmolested. They were declared innocent of any crime."

Heb. 4:14-16 (NIV):

> "Therefore, since we have a great high priest who has ascended into heaven, Jesus the Son of God, let us hold firmly to the faith we profess. For we do not have a high priest who is unable to empathize with our weaknesses, but we have one who has been tempted in every way, just as we are-yet he did not sin. Let us then approach God's throne of grace with confidence, so that we may receive mercy and find grace to help us in our time of need."

Wow. Jesus My High Priest. YES.
So much better to

> "TRUST in you to save me" (TPT)

and

> "take REFUGE in the Lord." (NIV). (Capitals mine.)

In summary I flip to the beginning of my two journals that I wrote my 31-day journey in and I discover a few notes and an old poem I wrote a few years back and it feels fitting to end this book....at the beginning.

"EVERYTHING FATHER.
Everything always seems to come back to Father (Father/Mother).
For years I've tried to access Papa by bypassing Jesus.
His Righteousness. My Righteousness.
I never felt worthy. Or enough.
When I asked Him (after listening to Graham Cooke),

Passover 2021

"Who do you want to be for me in this time?"

He replied,

"Everything".

I have been

- learning to ASK (Jer. 33:3)
- discovering PROVISION (You Promised to Take Care of Me)
- experiencing SAFETY (Ps. 91. You Cover me, You Carry me, You Care for me.)
- rewriting my story with HIS-STORY (No longer illegitimate but chosen IN HIM before the foundation of the world-His timeline written upon mine.)

And in all that

- accepting the invitation to LIVE (I will not die but live. Sleeping parts AWAKE and dead parts LIVE. John 10:10 [TPT] "I have come to give you everything in abundance, more than you expect-life in its fullness until you overflow!")

You are ALWAYS Speaking. To Me.
Having been surrounded by male figures throughout my life that don't often engage me in conversation or seem to have any desire to draw me out of me it is hard to believe and actively remember YOU WANT TO SPEAK TO ME.
Always.
You always have something to say to me.
You are continually/continuously thinking about me.
Dreaming of all I can have and do.
Waiting with Wisdom and Secrets and Mind Blowing Truths for me to just ASK.

Like a waterfall is a constant stream of many water droplets never letting up or faltering but faithfully pouring, falling, so are Your Words to me.
You never run out of words to speak to my heart.
You don't run dry.
You even cause water to flow from a rock. A rock!
You stop at nothing and nothing stops you.

Father May I?

I'm worth Your Investment.
You know it.
I must know it.
Your thoughts toward me outnumber the sand.

The Sky(e)'s the Limit.
Carefree and Weightless.
I am Your Joy"

~Such a Daddy's Girl~

The Dance by Skye Wright - 2017

I want increased hunger
I want increased desire
I want to break out of this rut
And into the fire

    Come dance with me
    To the rhythms of grace
    Let me gaze into your eyes
    Let me look upon your face

Lord you've had me from the start
But all this time I couldn't see
That your fiery heart of passion
Is consuming all of me

So I dance the dance of surrender
With the One whom my heart loves
Yes I dance the dance with my treasure
He is My Lover, I am His Dove

Together we go forward
Breaking out of what once was
And as we dance we conquer
And our weapon is our love

    For I've loved you from before time
    Yes I chose you to be mine
    So come dance our dance Beloved
    It is NOW   It is TIME

    Forever is our encore
    And our song brings all delight
    Come dance the dance of surrender
    All day long   Into the night

Want More?

Follow Skye on her upward journey at
https://upwards.ca
or scan the QR code below.

About the Author

Skye Wright is a woman on a journey of becoming more and more like a child every day. Born and raised a mountain girl, she loves small town life in the Kootenays, British Columbia and lives on the side of a mountain alongside all sorts of wildlife. An avid journaller since she was 10, she is never far from paper and pen and finds her heart comes alive most immersed in nature, exploring the earth or having fun with her family. Mom to her 7 greatest treasures and married to the love of her life for 20 years she has found the golden secret that a mundane life is an oxymoron for any Jesus Lover.

(Mundane: unimaginative, common, relating to this world as contrasted with heaven...in other words 'boring!') (www.dictionary.com)

Her ask of her Heavenly Papa when she got married was, "Please, let my life be anything but boring!"
And not only has Papa, yet again, come through, but she has discovered it is truly a Great Daring Adventure.
The cry of her heart as a child - for adventure - is finally being realized.
As well as riding her motorcycle and answering the call of the ocean whenever she gets the chance, writing this, her first book, has been one of her favorite adventures thus far and she is over the moon to share it with you.

www.ingramcontent.com/pod-product-compliance
Lightning Source LLC
Chambersburg PA
CBHW030325100526
44592CB00010B/570